RECENT REVOLUTIONS
IN ASTRONOMY

RECENT REVOLUTIONS
IN ASTRONOMY
Larry Kelsey
and
Darrel Hoff

FRANKLIN WATTS 1987
NEW YORK LONDON
TORONTO SYDNEY
A SCIENCE IMPACT BOOK

Diagrams by Vantage Art, Inc.

Photographs courtesy of Department of Library Services, American
Museum of Natural History: pp. 10 (#2A2361-top middle), 59
(#119137); Harvard College Observatory: p. 10 (top right and
bottom left); AT&T Bell Laboratories: pp. 10 (bottom middle),
14; Caltech photo by Robert Paz: p. 10 (bottom right); NASA:
pp. 17, 22, 27, 32, 34, 37, 41, 46, 67, 98, 116; NARO/AUI: p. 18;
Palomar Observatory photograph: pp. 24, 74, 87; Jet Propulsion
Laboratory: pp. 30, 31, 43, 48, 51; University of Arizona photo,
courtesy of Harold J. Reitsema: p. 52; Mount Wilson and Las
Campanas Observatories of the Carnegie Institution of Washington:
pp. 56, 91; National Optical Astronomy Observatories: pp. 61, 75,
88, 106, 109; The Yerkes Observatory: pp. 10 (top left), 78, 79,
80, 99; Lick Observatory, University of California: p. 103;
Maarten Schmidt, California Institute of Technology: p. 110.

Library of Congress Cataloging-in-Publication Data

Kelsey, Larry.
Recent revolutions in astronomy.

(A Science impact book)
Bibliography: p.
Includes index.
Summary: Discusses how recent innovations such as the
new telescopes are affecting the study of astronomy, our
understanding of the universe, and the search for new
galaxies and the origins of life.
1. Astronomy—Juvenile literature. [1. Astronomy.
2. Outer space—Exploration] I. Hoff, Darrel B.
II. Title. III. Series.
QB46.K37 1987   520   86-23340
ISBN 0-531-10340-4

CONTENTS

7122179

*THIS BOOK IS FOR TWO
WHOSE LOVE AND SUPPORT HELPED
MAKE IT POSSIBLE—OUR WIVES,
ANNE AND ARDITH*

REVOLUTIONS
IN ASTRONOMY

Before 1543, the word *revolution* had only one meaning: the act of orbiting something, as in "The moon makes one revolution around the earth each month."

But in that year the Polish astronomer Nicolaus Copernicus published a book entitled *On the Revolutions of the Celestial Spheres,* which set forth the startling theory that the earth orbited the sun. Soon almost everyone was talking about Copernicus's "revolutionary" book.

Within a short time the word *revolution* had taken on a new meaning. People used it to mean any surprisingly new way to think about or do something. A revolution represented a complete change or a break with the past.

Sometimes a revolution is violent, as in the American Revolution, with its Battles of Lexington and Concord, or the French Revolution, with the bloody guillotine. Other times it is a peaceful act, as in a revolution in thought. This happens when a new idea replaces an older one, because the older one is not as good at describing something. It is this second type of revolution that we will be discussing in this book.

Since he accidentally redefined the word, the honor of the first modern revolution in science has to go to Copernicus.

But this revolution was not complete until 1609, when the Italian astronomer Galileo Galilei discovered that the planet Venus had phases like those of the moon. This could happen *only* if Venus goes around the Sun. How did Galileo make this discovery? With a telescope. Galileo was the first to use this new piece of equipment in the study of astronomy.

THE CAMERA
CHANGES ASTRONOMY

Another revolution in astronomy, even though it began more than a century ago, was centered around the use of the camera by astronomers. The science of photography began with a few crude images recorded on metallic plates in the 1830s. It didn't take astronomers long to realize that photography would prove useful in studying the heavens. In fact, the first known photograph taken through a telescope was made in 1840. It was a 30-minute exposure of the moon.

As cameras and films improved, astronomers began photographing the entire sky, not just bright objects like the sun, moon, and planets. This was a better way of mapping the sky than drawing it by hand. Soon there were a number of photographic atlases, or directories, of the stars. Such atlases allowed astronomers to precisely determine the positions of the stars and planets. Determining the distances to the nearest stars then became fairly easy.

Determining distances has always been one of the most critical and difficult problems in astronomy. Knowing astronomical distances enables one to calculate the extent of the Milky Way galaxy and see how the Milky Way compares in size to the other galaxies.

Before the camera was introduced into the science of astronomy, the distances to only fifty-five stars had been measured. More than six thousand stellar distances were determined using photographic techniques over the next seventy years.

Photography has also revolutionized the way *asteroids* are discovered. Asteroids are miniature planets usually found between the orbits of Mars and Jupiter. The first asteroid was found in 1801. Other asteroids were discovered from time to time, until three hundred were known in 1891. But in that year, the German astronomer Max Wolf began to use photography to discover them. Today more than three thousand asteroids are known.

LARGE TELESCOPES

Two well-known twentieth-century American astronomers are Harlow Shapley and Edwin Hubble. They are remembered for their part in another revolution. Shapley helped to locate the sun's place in the Milky Way galaxy. Hubble helped to show that millions of galaxies exist. His work also led to the revolutionary idea that the universe is expanding, and that it was "born" billions of years ago in the "big bang."

How was this revolution possible? Of course it required the brilliant minds of these astronomers as well as others, but it was largely made possible by the use of large telescopes.

Before 1917, the biggest telescope lens in the world had a diameter of 60 inches (1.5 meters). But in that year, the new 100-inch (2.5-meter) telescope on Mount Wilson, in southern California, came into service. It could gather almost three times more light than the 60-inch (1.5-meter) telescope. Over the next few years, Shapley and Hubble used this new telescope to see fainter stars and galaxies more clearly than anyone before them had done. This telescope, and the astronomers who used it, truly revolutionized how we view our universe.

RECENT REVOLUTIONS

There have been many revolutions in astronomy. Some have depended on new equipment or technology. Examples of this technology include radio telescopes, telescopes that "see" infrared and ultraviolet light, spacecraft, computers, and observatories that orbit the earth, above our atmosphere.

Some revolutions were launched by certain individuals with an innovative insight, or a different way of looking at the facts. Examples of these revolutions are Albert Einstein's discovery of relativity, Maarten Schmidt's understanding of the radiation emitted by quasars, and Stephen Hawking's discoveries about black holes.

Regardless of the type of discovery, the science of astronomy has undergone startling changes within the last couple of decades. For example, there was a time when a solitary astronomer sat behind his or her telescope night after night charting and photographing the heavens. This is no longer true.

Today astronomers work in teams, spread across the nation, if not the world. Many study the sky during the day

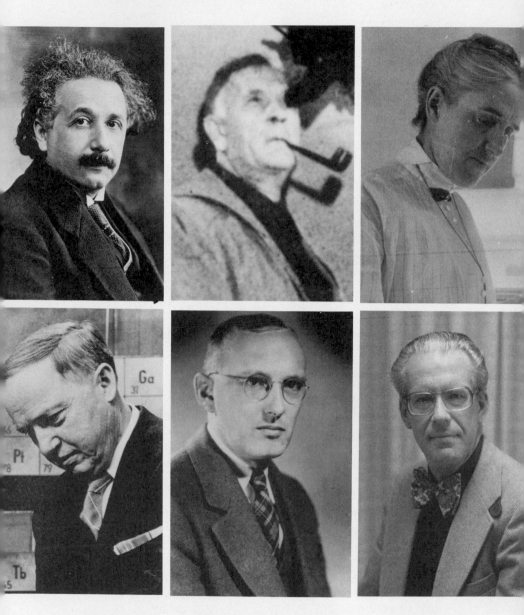

Top (from left to right): Albert Einstein, Edwin Hubble, Henrietta S. Leavitt. Bottom (from left to right): Harlow Shapley, Karl Jansky, Maarten Schmidt—six pioneers of modern astronomy

rather than the night. They acquire their data with multimillion-dollar instruments that hardly resemble telescopes. Then they sift their data through computers that can make millions of comparisons of pieces of information each second. And they work hand in hand with physicists, biologists, chemists, and engineers.

It is a big enterprise. Then again, the universe is a big subject. And most of these people began their journey in the same way that you have likely begun, by looking up at the night sky and wondering. Then, perhaps, someone showed these scientists a small telescope and they began to discover.

The revolutions in astronomy are far from finished. As long as there are new minds and new tools, they will continue to occur. We would like you to be a part of these revolutions.

CHAPTER 1
THE NEW TELESCOPES

F or most of history, humans have studied the sky with the instruments they were born with—their eyes. About 400 years ago, however, the Italian astronomer Galileo Galilei showed the world a new way to explore the heavens—with the telescope. Thus was born a major revolution in astronomy.

For three and a half centuries the telescope remained the most important tool of the astronomer, and the goal of the astronomer was to build bigger and more sensitive telescopes. Through them astronomers were able to see further and more clearly than ever before.

But within the last half century or so, another major revolution has occurred. Today we are aware that the heavens shine not only in light that we can see with our eyes, but also in light that is visible only to special detectors.

Suddenly there are new fields of study with names like radio astronomy, X-ray astronomy, and gamma-ray astronomy. These areas have produced many of the most startling discoveries that astronomers have ever made.

JANSKY DISCOVERS
RADIO ASTRONOMY

The story begins in 1931 with a scientist named Karl Jansky, who was working for Bell Telephone Laboratories in New Jersey, trying to track down the source of some static that interfered with radio transmissions.

He had built a house-size construction of wires and lumber, which was his radio antenna. With it, he discovered that

Karl Jansky was using this antenna when he accidentally detected radio waves coming from space.

certain types of static were not human made, but rather came from beyond the earth. This was the birth of radio astronomy. Jansky's antenna was actually receiving radio energy from the center of our galaxy!

A *radio telescope,* which is what we now call the device Jansky built, is similar to an ordinary radio receiver. The basic differences are that radio telescopes are much more sensitive and are tuned to different "stations." They don't pick up music or the ball game. They pick up the noise created by stars, planets, galaxies, and large clouds of gas in space.

Most of us have seen pictures of huge, dish-shaped radio telescopes. These are the superstars of radio astronomy. They collect the radio signals in much the same way that ordinary (optical) telescopes gather light. The signals strike the dish-shaped antenna, which focuses them on a receiver in front of the dish. From there the signal is sent to a computer. As the dish moves back and forth across the source, the computer builds up an image, eventually creating a picture of the object detected by the radio telescope.

Other radio telescopes look nothing like huge dishes. Some consist of wires strung across a field, or springlike coils of metal tubing. They pick up radio signals just like the straight or coiled wire attached to your portable radio. And with them, astronomers have created a new window to the universe.

At first, Jansky's surprising discovery did not lead to an explosion of radio telescope construction. Most astronomers saw the radio telescope as a curiosity, not a tool with which they could examine the universe. Only after World War II, when money had been put into the development of radio and radar for wartime purposes, did scientists begin to see the possibilities for radio telescopes. Following the war, many of these radio/radar devices were turned over to the scientists for them to experiment with.

These radio telescopes have truly created a revolution in modern astronomy. Take, for example, the study of supernovas. A supernova occurs when a massive star blows itself up at the end of its life. (More will be said about this process in Chapter 5.) In all of recorded history, only about half a dozen supernovas had been seen in our galaxy. And none have been sighted in almost 400 years! Their rarity made them hard to study.

Radio astronomers have found that their telescopes can detect the remnants of supernovas that either were too dim to see or happened before recorded history. In this manner, dozens of ancient supernovas have been found. Studying these remnants has helped us to better understand how often supernovas occur and how they affect our galaxy.

For about 20 years, astronomers built larger and larger radio antennas. This allowed them to see fainter objects, farther away. But eventually the instruments became too big to be easily movable, and sometimes too expensive to build.

Currently the largest fully steerable radio dish is in Bonn, Germany, and is 330 feet (100 meters) in diameter. A fully steerable radio telescope dish can be pointed at all times to anywhere in the sky. Partially steerable telescopes have limited scanning ability and are often usable only when directly facing the place in the sky that the astronomer wants to study. Larger radio telescopes have been built, but they are only partially steerable. The biggest of these is the 1,000-foot (305-meter) dish at Arecibo Observatory in Puerto Rico. It is unlikely that we will see radio dishes larger than this, because we now have a better way to improve the resolving power of a radio telescope. It involves a technique known as *interferometry.*

INTERFEROMETRY: TWO IS BETTER THAN ONE

Interferometry simulates a large antenna by using two or more smaller antennas. The two radio dishes are placed some distance apart and pointed toward a radio source. The waves from the source strike one antenna a brief instant before striking the other. This means the two antennas will receive the same waves at slightly different times so that the waves become out of phase with each other. The difference in phase between the waves depends on the angle the source makes with a line between the antennas. Determining this angle enables astronomers to pinpoint the position of the source in the sky.

This setup, called an interferometer, can pinpoint exact source locations better than ordinary radio telescopes. Although radio telescopes can be very sensitive, detecting extremely faint sources, they have poor "eyesight," what astronomers call *resolution.* They cannot easily be used to determine exactly which star (or other object) is broadcasting.

For example, in the early 1960s when the stellar objects called quasars were discovered, it could not be determined exactly which of many stars in a particular area was creating the radio noise. Only when interferometers began to be used could the sources be identified with known stars. Then they could be studied with optical telescopes. This led to our solving the riddle of quasars. (More on this in Chapter 7.)

The 1000-foot (305-meter) radio/radar antenna
at the Arecibo Observatory in Puerto Rico. When
the dish is operating as a receiver, radio waves from
space are collected by the reflector and focused
on the antenna suspended above the center. They
are then relayed to monitors in the control center.

The distance between the interferometer's two dishes is called the baseline. The larger the baseline, the more accurately we can locate the direction of the source. Suppose the two antennas are 1 mile (1.6 kilometers) apart. We can reproduce the resolving power of a single telescope dish 1 mile (1.6 kilometers) in diameter with our interferometer. Of course, it will not have the sensitivity of a single telescope with such a diameter, because it cannot gather nearly as much radio energy. But it will be able to resolve objects the way such a single larger instrument could.

Radio astronomers quickly realized that there was no limit to the length of the baseline between the antennas. In a short time, interferometers comprising a number of telescopes spread over larger and larger distances were operating. Currently, the world's most impressive telescope array is the Very Large Array (VLA) near Socorro, New Mexico. The

Several antennas that are part of the Very Large Array radio telescope near Socorro, New Mexico. The VLA has twenty-seven antennas in all, which can be moved along railroad tracks as necessary.

VLA, completed in 1980, has twenty-seven telescopes, each with a diameter of 82 feet (25 meters), which can be moved along rails laid out in a large Y shape covering 22 miles (36 kilometers) of the desert!

The largest baseline that astronomers have used so far is approximately the diameter of the earth—8,000 miles (13,000 kilometers). This was accomplished by hooking up an antenna in the United States with one in Australia. Imagine the difficulty involved in simultaneously using radio telescopes on opposite sides of the planet!

In the future, astronomers expect to see even larger separations. The only requirement is a radio dish in space. With such an instrument, we could have million-mile (1.6-million-kilometer) baselines! In a decade or two, space interferometers will undoubtedly allow us to look into the secrets of our universe.

OTHER WAVELENGTHS

Light is more properly known to astronomers as *electromagnetic radiation,* that is, energy that results from oscillating electric and magnetic fields. Depending upon its wavelength, this radiation is detectable as visible light, X-rays, gamma rays, ultraviolet light, infrared light, or radio. All these forms of energy make up the *electromagnetic spectrum*.

Only radio waves and visible light can easily pass through the earth's atmosphere. That is why radio and optical astronomy developed first. Lately, however, other regions of the electromagnetic spectrum have come under increasing study. One of these regions is the infrared.

Infrared radiation has just slightly longer wavelengths than does visible light. Infrared radiation is the energy we usually experience as heat. All astronomical objects give off infrared light, even those invisible to our eyes. So if we can view the heavens with our infrared detectors, we can often catch a glimpse of things otherwise invisible. The trouble is that most of this infrared radiation is prevented from reaching our telescopes by the gases in our atmosphere. Some infrared does manage to make it through our atmosphere, so infrared astronomy can be done at a few major observatories

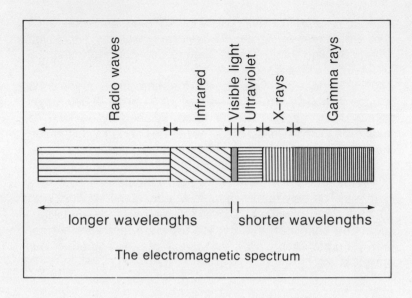

The electromagnetic spectrum

located on mountains high above the thickest part of our air. Mauna Kea Observatory, in Hawaii, the highest observatory in the world at 13,800 feet (4,200 meters), has several large telescopes dedicated to infrared work. The large instrument operated on Mount Jelm, Wyoming, by the University of Wyoming is also observing in the infrared. But these are the exceptions. The easiest place to do infrared astronomy is from space.

In 1983, the Infrared Astronomical Satellite (IRAS) was launched into earth orbit. It contained a 22.4-inch (57-centimeter) infrared telescope to examine the heavens. In order to keep the telescope from detecting its own infrared emissions, it had to be cooled to −455 degrees Fahrenheit (−271 degrees Celsius) by liquid helium. Think of how hard it is to start a car, or to run any other machine, at temperatures a little below freezing. Now imagine building a telescope to operate at nearly *absolute zero,* the lowest possible temperature!

The end of the mission occurred when the coolant ran out after ten months, but during that time the satellite was one of the most productive spacecraft ever launched. Its detectors were so sensitive that they could find a speck of dust at a distance of 2 miles (3.2 kilometers). While in operation, IRAS discovered five new comets, a minor planet, and more than two hundred thousand other far-infrared point sources. One of the most interesting finds was the discovery that a number of nearby stars are surrounded by a cool cloud of solid particles. These may represent planetary systems in the process of forming.

The success of this satellite has led to anticipation of the results from the Shuttle Infrared Telescope Facility, which will contain a 33.5-inch (85-centimeter) infrared telescope and will be flown aboard the space shuttle.

Ultraviolet radiation is another part of the spectrum that has a difficult time getting through our atmosphere. This is good for us, since a little ultraviolet gives us a tan, but a lot can kill us. The ultraviolet astronomers, however, have to lift their instruments above the atmosphere in order to study the "ultraviolet universe"—the universe seen in ultraviolet radiation only.

A number of ultraviolet satellites have been launched. The Orbiting Astronomical Observatory (named after Copernicus) was the first in orbit in 1972. This was followed by the European satellite TD-1 in 1974. But the most successful of the space satellites was the International Ultraviolet Explorer (IUE) launched in 1978. IUE carried a 17.7-inch (45-centimeter) telescope capable of creating a televisionlike image of the sky in the ultraviolet, and enabling some sources invisible to our eyes to be examined.

Electromagnetic energy with wavelengths even shorter than ultraviolet is called *X-radiation,* (better known as *X-rays*). The X-ray sky is also not visible from the surface of the earth since X-rays are absorbed by our atmosphere. But since 1962, detectors flown on rockets, balloons, and satellites have studied the X-rays from celestial objects.

The most recent X-ray telescopes placed into orbit were the HEAO 1 and HEAO 2 (HEAO is short for High Energy Astronomical Observatory). The second, launched in 1978, contained a 22-inch (56-centimeter) X-ray telescope and was known as the Einstein Observatory.

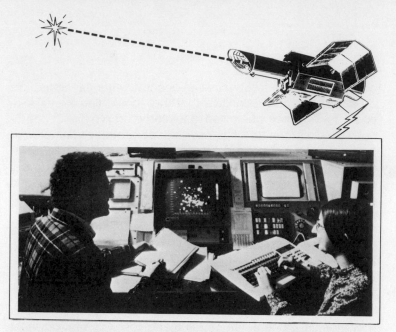

These astronomers are working with data gathered by the orbiting International Ultraviolet Explorer. Ultraviolet light is gathered by the telescope and the data transmitted to the NASA Goddard Space Flight Center in Greenbelt, Maryland, and to an identical center in Madrid, Spain.

X-rays are not easy to bring to a focus to form a picture. They usually go through things or are absorbed by surfaces. In order to make an image, the telescope had to be made differently. The X-ray telescope contained a number of nested cones made of metal. X-rays would enter the telescope, glance off of the surfaces of these cones at a shallow (1°) angle, and be brought to focus on an X-ray detector.

Both HEAO 1 and 2 made extensive measurements of a number of objects of interest to astronomers, for example, the center of our galaxy, which is an extremely powerful X-ray emitter. These satellites have determined how powerful an emitter it is and helped us to understand the way the energy is produced. They have also observed pulsars and suspected black holes.

The electromagnetic radiation with the shortest wavelength is known as *gamma rays*. Gamma ray astronomy is also an activity best conducted above the earth's atmosphere. It first became known that some objects emit bursts of gamma rays when by accident a U.S. satellite (*Vela*) measured such a burst. The satellite had been launched to look for nuclear weapons tests on earth.

Since that time, a half dozen different satellites from a number of countries have made gamma ray measurements. The design of these telescopes is quite similar to that of the X-ray telescopes.

Objects that produce gamma rays are nearly always X-ray emitters as well, so in most cases gamma ray astronomers are studying galactic nuclei, pulsars, and black holes. We will talk more about these objects in Chapters 5 and 6.

THE NEW OPTICAL TELESCOPES

For three decades after 1948, the largest optical telescope in the world was the 200-inch (5-meter) Hale telescope on Palomar Mountain in southern California. Many astronomers felt that larger instruments would just be a waste of money and time, since the earth's atmosphere limits a telescope's powers of resolution. But if you could lift the telescopes above the atmosphere, then larger telescopes would make sense. However, recent technological and scientific advances have caused astronomers to reexamine the problem. As a result, many huge earth-bound telescopes are now in the planning or construction stages.

INTERPRETING STAR SPECKLES

The first breakthrough leading to huge telescopes involved something called speckle interferometry. At any instant, the image of a star looks speckled because different parts of that image are affected by the slightly different paths that light has taken through our atmosphere before it came together in the image. A long photographic exposure blurs these speckles into a fuzzy disk, which is what we see when we photograph a star.

Speckle interferometry involves very short exposure times on the order of 1/50 of a second. Mathematical techniques and a computer are then used to deduce the proper-

ties of the starlight that entered the telescope. A detailed image is formed by superimposing a number of these photographs on one another. In this way, the computer assembles a photograph of the star. This process can allow us to measure the star's size or even show us markings on its surface.

This technique has been used on a number of objects and shows promise for a way of getting around some of the blurring effects of our atmosphere.

FAT MIRRORS MADE THIN

The largest optical telescope in the world is the 236-inch (6-meter) instrument at the Crimean Astrophysical Observatory in the Soviet Union. The problems involved in making a mirror this large are staggering. This particular one weighs 42 tons (almost 38,000 kilograms) and is more than 2 feet (65 centimeters) thick. After the mirror was poured, it took a *year* to cool slowly and nearly *six years* to grind and polish! The supporting and tracking systems had to be extremely powerful, yet delicate enough to move this monster accurately by tiny increments.

One way to simplify the mirror-making process is to make the mirror thinner. If carefully supported from the back, a thin but large mirror will not crack. This requires sensitive monitoring and adjusting of tensions by a computer, but it can be done. The University of Texas is currently exploring this design for a 23-foot (7-meter) mirror that would be only a couple of inches thick (less than 10 centimeters).

Another method is to make the mirror partially hollow. Experiments at the University of Arizona have shown that hundreds of drinking-glass-size cells can be fused together to form a surface that has the appearance of a honeycomb. This reduces the mirror weight while preserving much of the structural strength, allowing for the creation of really big mirrors.

The 200-inch (5-meter) Hale telescope
on Palomar Mountain in California

A third alternative involves segmented or multiple mirrors. In the 1970s the University of Arizona built the Multiple Mirror Telescope (MMT). It was made from six 71-inch (1.8 meter) mirrors, harnessed together into a single telescope. The individual mirrors have their light focused together into one image by a laser-controlled optics system.

Scientists are attempting to extend this concept to much larger designs. For instance, the University of California is working on a 33-foot (10-meter) segmented-mirror instrument which will have sixty 55-inch (1.4 meter) hexagons fused into one mirror. The mirror's thickness would be only 4 inches (10 centimeters). The site planned for this telescope is the top of Mauna Kea, Hawaii. Construction began in September 1985, with the date of completion set for 1990.

Kitt Peak National Observatory, in Arizona, has already announced plans for a 50-foot (15-meter) segmented telescope, also to be built on Mauna Kea. Where will it all end?

SPACE TELESCOPE

The telescope that may truly revolutionize astronomy in this decade is the Hubble Space Telescope (HST), which is the product of more than 20 years of planning. Though a modest 94 inches (2.4 meters) in diameter, it represents the leading edge of today's science and technology. The planned launch date for this instrument was to have been autumn of 1986, but as of the writing of this book, the project is on hold because of a halt in shuttle flights.

Its location in space, high above the murky atmosphere, will enable astronomers to detect objects fainter and farther away than those detectable by any other telescope—fifty times fainter and seven times farther. You can get an idea of its resolving power by the following example. If the HST were above New York City, it could resolve the headlights of a car over San Francisco! That is five times better resolution than the best ground-based telescope could achieve under ideal weather conditions!

The HST has five major instruments to study the heavens. There is the High Speed Photometer, which measures the amount of light sent to us from faint objects, and can do it

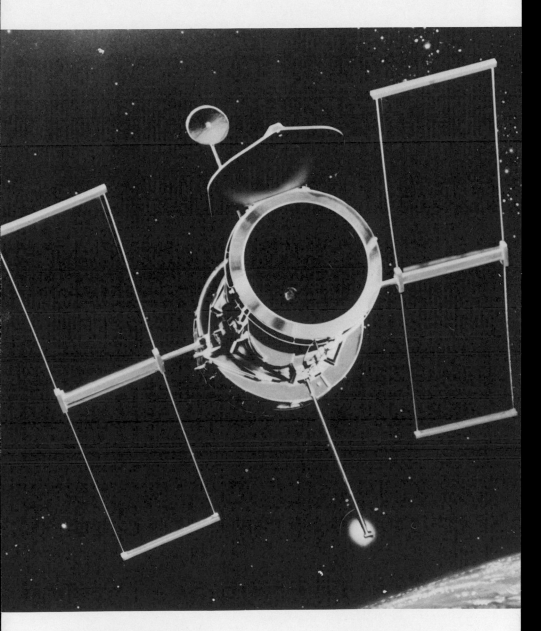

*An artist's conception of
the space telescope orbiting earth*

up to a hundred thousand times per second! Now we can look for stars that have very rapid light fluctuations. This is something we can't do from the surface of the earth.

There are two instruments aboard to analyze the radiation emitted from various objects. The High Resolution Spectrograph can take the light from a star or galaxy and spread it out into a very long and detailed spectrum. Much of this instrument's work will be an extension of the IUE satellite's successes. The Faint-Object Spectrograph produces smaller spectra but has to be able to work with much dimmer objects. (See Chapter 4 for information on spectra and spectrographs.)

A device that can photograph extremely dim stars, called the Faint-Object Camera, is also aboard. This instrument might even be able to detect planets around other stars.

And finally, there is the Wide-Field/Planetary Camera, to be used to examine closer and brighter objects (like planets and moons), or those that are not point sources but are somewhat extended (like galaxies or nebulas).

The whole assembly is 43.5 feet (13 meters) long and 14 feet (4.3 meters) in diameter, about the size of a small house trailer. It weighs 25,500 pounds (11,600 kilograms), of which 1,800 pounds (820 kilograms) is the mirror! The HST is one of the heaviest scientific payloads ever placed into orbit.

Over the next few years of its operation, the HST is expected to help us better understand the nature of quasars, perhaps see planets around nearby stars, determine whether the universe will expand forever, and answer many other questions. As happens with any new technological advance, there undoubtedly will be many unexpected discoveries as well.

At its altitude of 310 miles (500 kilometers), the HST is expected to have a lifetime of about 15 years, so astronomers are looking forward to using the HST into the first few years of the twenty-first century. By that time its status as the largest orbiting telescope will probably have been surpassed by newer instruments.

CHAPTER 2
NEIGHBORING
WORLDS

*U*ntil fairly recently, most of the planets and all of the moons in our Solar System were little more than dots on an astronomer's photographic plate. We imagined what we might see if we could stand on the surface of Mars as a raging dust storm approached, or orbited above Jupiter's Great Red Spot, staring down into that huge pink eye. Today we can visit these and other worlds through the robot eyes of spacecraft with names like *Viking, Voyager,* and *Venera.* In the decades ahead, when humans finally journey in person to these worlds, their destinations will be known, recognizable places, due to the efforts of these mechanical scouts.

MERCURY: HOT DAYS
AND COLD NIGHTS

Up until 1965, little was known about the physical appearance of the planet Mercury. Astronomers knew it had the shortest year of any planet (88 days), that it orbited the sun at an average distance of 36 million miles (58 million kilometers), and that it had a diameter of about 3,000 miles (4,800 kilometers). The only thing we knew about its appearance was that there were some large dark areas here and there on the planet.

Observations of Mercury from Earth are difficult. Since it is never seen to be more than 28 degrees from the sun, it is always viewed in the sun's glare. In fact, this planet is so hard to see that many well-known astronomers—including Copernicus—never observed it. As a result, even with the largest telescopes, astronomers were unable to determine accurate-

Left: The launching of Voyager 1
Above: One of the Voyager probes

The surface of Mercury, photographed by Mariner 10 *in 1974 at a distance of 49,000 miles (78,000 kilo-meters). The "tear" in the surface of the planet at the upper left was caused by a loss of data during transmission of the picture.*

ly the length of Mercury's day by timing the rotation of a dark surface spot.

In 1965, astronomers first bounced radar waves off Mercury using the large Arecibo radio telescope dish. This allowed them to determine the speed of rotation of Mercury in a way quite similar to the method used by police to measure the speed of a passing car. This is done by calculating the *Doppler shift* of the radio waves.

You may have heard the pitch of a car horn drop as the car speeds past you. That is because the sound waves are stretched out from the receding horn. This shift is a result of the *Doppler effect,* named after the Austrian physicist Christian Doppler, who first investigated the idea that sound would change its wavelength if its source was moving. Later it was found that all electromagnetic waves exhibited the Doppler effect as well.

The Doppler shift that astronomers found was a bit surprising, indicating a rotational period of 58.6 Earth days. It was thought that Mercury would probably rotate in 88 Earth days, keeping one face to the sun. But this was not the case.

Little additional information about Mercury was discovered over the next decade. Then in 1974 a spacecraft named *Mariner 10* sent us back a wealth of new data. *Mariner* had been sent to pass by Venus and then to make not one but three separate flybys of Mercury. In the first-ever close-up pictures of the planet that resulted from the mission, scientists discovered scenes that reminded them of our moon. Thouasands of craters, some hundreds of miles across, can be seen. There are even large basins, similar to lunar basins with their dark, smooth floors.

We now have a fairly complete picture of the scene that will greet any future space travelers who may be so "fortunate" as to stand upon the surface of Mercury. They will need space suits, since there is a nearly undetectable, thin atmosphere. And they will have to be better insulated than the *Apollo* astronauts who visited the moon. Mercury is about three times closer to the sun, and therefore much hotter than the moon. In fact, daytime temperatures can reach 800 degrees Fahrenheit (430 degrees Celsius). Not only would the days be hot, they would be long—88 Earth days. The night would be just as long and frighteningly cold at −279 degrees Fahrenheit (−173 degrees Celsius). Although the scene would look quite similar to that on the moon, with craters and a dusty surface, our explorers would also notice that they weigh twice what they would on the moon, or a third of their earth weight.

All in all, it is quite a desolate and uncomfortable picture. Yet, it seems possible that the next century will find a mining or scientific colony located on the planet. This is something that will probably *not* occur on the second planet from the sun, Venus.

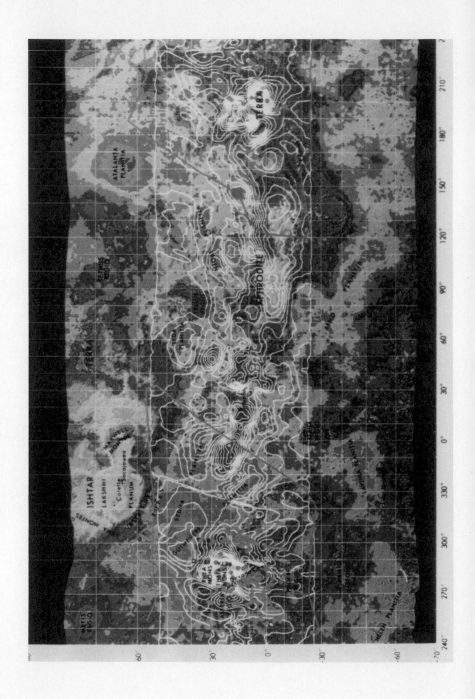

VENUS: THE CAULDRON

Our knowledge of Venus closely parelleled that of Mercury until the mid-1960s. It, too, is seen only close to the sun. But Venus is surrounded by a layer of clouds so thick that no one had ever been able to view any feature on the surface of the planet.

Until the beginning of the 1960s, Venus was often regarded as the Earth's twin. It is our closest neighbor planet, and it is about the same size and density as the Earth. It's closer to the sun, but its thick blanket of clouds probably reflects much of that energy. Therefore, we might expect it to have a temperature like Earth's. Venus was also known to have an atmosphere with some of the gases found in our own atmosphere.

Those who thought Venus was another Earth were thoroughly startled by facts discovered during the last two decades. It now appears that Venus resembles the classical description of hell more than anything else!

Once again, it was radar that began to open our eyes. In the early 1960s, radar was bounced off the planet. Two surprises resulted. The planet was found to have a rotational period of 243 earth days—longer than its year. *And* it rotated backward. This last fact makes it unique among the planets in the Solar System.

Because of Venus's dense clouds, radar has become the chief instrument for exploring the planet. Over the years, both Earth-based and Venus-orbiting radar units have mapped the planet with greater and greater accuracy. Venus is largely covered with flat, rolling plains. There are, however, some highland and lowland areas. The highlands are almost

Radar map of Venus. Two features are of particular interest: Beta Regio and Aphrodite Terra—two suspected volcanic areas. The gray dots in these areas represent lightning, which is practically continuous on the planet.

like continents on the Earth, except that there is no liquid water on Venus.

More than twenty spacecraft have been sent by the United States and the Soviet Union to explore the planet. The Soviet *Venera* series of spacecraft have sent us the only pictures, thus far, of the surface. They show a rocky surface that seems to have weathered very little. The spacecraft only worked for a few minutes before breaking down. The reason is the harsh environment of Venus.

We now know that the clouds are made up of drops of sulfuric acid, not water drops like here on Earth. The surface pressure is extremely high, more than ninety times greater than our atmospheric pressure. This means the air is much thicker on Venus. Walking around on the surface of Venus would be similar to trying to walk around on the floor of Earth's oceans 1 mile (1.6 kilometers) down. And the temperature is about 900 degrees Fahrenheit (about 480 degrees Celsius), hot enough to melt lead and glass. Imagine the difficulty of making a machine that could withstand this sort of environment! This is why it looks unlikely that humans will walk upon the surface of Venus in the foreseeable future.

OUR MOON:
NO GREEN CHEESE!

For countless centuries, humans have gazed up at the moon, wondering about its nature and even fantasizing about journeys to it. Four hundred years ago the famous German astronomer Johannes Kepler, in what some people believe was the first science fiction story, wrote about an imaginary trip to the moon.

For many years people nourished superstitions and strange fantasies about the moon: the moon was made of green cheese; it was where lost articles went; moonlight made you crazy; living creatures existed there. But after Galileo first pointed his telescope at the moon in 1609, these notions began to die out, to be replaced by facts. The moon was a world, in some ways like the earth. There were mountains, craters, and broad, flat areas called *maria,* since they

*Astronaut Harrison H. Schmitt on the moon
during the mission of* Apollo 17 *in 1972*

looked like seas. *Maria,* pronounced MAR-ee-a, is the Latin word for "seas."

However, we learned that these maria were not seas, since there was no water on the moon. This and the fact that the moon had no atmosphere seemed to rule out the possibility of life.

Still the moon interested astronomers. Where did it come from? Had it always orbited the earth? What was it made of? Certainly not green cheese, but were the rocks similar to earth rocks? These and other questions led scientists in the early 1960s to propose a visit to the moon.

From earth, we can see only one side of the moon. This is because the moon orbits our planet in a way that always keeps the same side toward us. Think of all the people throughout time who have looked at the moon and wondered what the other side looked like.

One of the first accomplishments of the space age was to photograph the backside of the moon. This was first done by a Soviet spacecraft in 1959. The pictures showed us a more rugged face than the near side, one that had few dark, smooth maria but many more craters. Scientists are still trying to understand why the moon's two sides are so different.

The decade that followed this discovery should probably be called the Lunar Decade. Dozens of spacecraft from the United States and the Soviet Union were sent to photograph, orbit, and analyze the moon. All of these robot spacecraft were in preparation for sending astronauts to the moon.

At first, these robot probes were intentionally crashed into the lunar surface. Most of them carried cameras that photographed right up to the moment of impact. Later, instruments were soft-landed. Some contained remote-controlled vehicles that explored the surface.

The high point of lunar exploration was the period from 1969 to 1972 when the United States, as part of the *Apollo* program, sent men to the moon. Many people who were around then can tell you where they were and what they were doing on the afternoon of July 20, 1969. It was an important moment in history—the first time humans had landed on another world.

There were five other landings during the next three years, taking ten more men to the surface of the moon. Equally important to accomplishing this feat were the scientific data that these missions returned to earth. Nearly a half ton (450 kilograms) of lunar material came back with the astronauts.

We now know that the moon has the same types of rocks found on earth. No new elements were expected to be discovered on the moon, and none were, although there are some small differences in the abundances of elements.

The astronauts left scientific monitoring stations on the moon after their visits. These operated for several years before running out of energy. Instruments on these stations have detected "moonquakes." But these are far less frequent and energetic than earthquakes.

Studying the signals from these moonquakes has told us much about the moon's interior. For one thing, we now suspect that the moon has a small molten core somewhat like the earth's. This is something that many scientists thought unlikely before the *Apollo* landings.

Something else that was confirmed came from the reflectors left at each landing site. By carefully aiming a laser at the lunar reflectors, a pulse of light can be sent to the moon and back. Noting the travel time of the light allows us to measure the distance to the moon with great accuracy. This has shown that the moon is slowly backing away from us by about 1 inch (2.5 centimeters) per year! Not much, but over millions (if not billions) of years, it becomes quite a lot. This was known from gravitational theory, but now we have the proof.

One of the questions that scientists wished to answer concerned the origin of the moon. Was the moon alongside the earth when the earth formed? Did it split from the earth? Was it captured as it passed by our planet?

The data from *Apollo* did not absolutely answer this question, and there is still considerable argument on the issue. Some astronomers today believe that the moon and the earth formed alongside each other. Others believe the moon resulted from the collision of a large asteroid and the earth, and this view is gaining support.

The moon has largely been ignored by the American and Soviet space programs since the last astronaut walked on the moon in 1972 (although scientists continue to study the lunar samples and data). But humans may soon return to the moon. Besides being a logical site for scientific study, the moon looks like the best source of raw material for our continued expansion into space. The twenty-first century will undoubtedly find more than one colony situated on the moon to exploit its resources.

MARS AND MARTIANS

Martians exist. They not only exist, they are or will soon be on Earth! The people who will live on and explore Mars in the twenty-first century may be among the youth of today. *They* are the first Martians.

A century ago, a number of people believed there might be a native race of Martians. They spoke of the similarities between Earth and Mars. Mars had a day that was only half an hour longer than Earth's. Mars had polar caps, like Earth. Mars was tilted on its axis to within 1.75 degrees of Earth's tilt. And Mars was seen to have clouds (though much thinner than Earth's). Then there were those "canals."

A few astronomers had reported viewing thin, dark, straight lines on the planet. These, they thought, were canals carrying water from the melting polar caps to the dry desert regions. And if there were canals, there must be Martians to build them. Although most astronomers did not see the canals, this did not stop many people from believing in Martians.

Gradually we began to understand the true nature of Mars, largely through the efforts of about a dozen spacecraft. What we found was discouraging to those looking for Martian life.

The first three spacecraft flew by the planet, photographing and measuring it on three occasions from 1965 to 1969. What they showed was a dead-looking world. Craters were all over the place. It appeared to be a red version of the moon. Later probes, sent to orbit the planet, showed us a much more active-looking world. There were deep canyons, sand dunes, dust storms, volcanoes, and dried-up stream beds—evidence of geologic life, if not biologic life.

Then, in 1976, two *Viking* spacecraft landed on Mars, sending back our first pictures of its surface. We now know the type of environment our future Martians will experience.

The temperature is normally quite cold. On a typical day it might be −10 degrees Fahrenheit (−23 degrees Celsius), falling to −190 degrees Fahrenheit (−123 degrees Celsius) during the night. Occasionally, during summer, the temperature might actually climb to a comfortable 80 degrees Fahr-

Mars photographed from the Viking 1 *orbiter on July 11, 1976, at a distance of 11,000 miles (18,000 kilometers) from the Martian surface*

enheit (26 degrees Celsius). Even then, our Martians wouldn't find themselves out sunning. The atmosphere is very thin—a hundred times thinner than ours. As a result, most of the sun's light would find its way to the planet's surface. Within 15 minutes, a person would be badly sunburned by the ultraviolet radiation. Longer exposures could kill any living thing!

The thin air is also not breathable. Since it is mostly carbon dioxide, we would need an oxygen mask if not an entire space suit.

Liquid water does not exist on Mars, but some of the polar cap is water ice. There also appears to be water frozen beneath the Martian surface, like the permafrost in our own Arctic regions. So we would have a source of water.

Sandstorms would present an occasional problem. Every couple of years they blanket the entire planet, hiding the sun for months at a time. Our Martian greenhouses had better have some emergency grow lights, for plants cannot go that long without sunlight.

Though Mars appears to be a world less than ideally suited to life, it does seem habitable. Undoubtedly it will be the next world to be visited by us. One day some of our descendants may well call it home.

JUPITER: THE GIANT PLANET

Jupiter is the giant of our Solar System—a world with a volume one thousand times that of Earth. It is a beautiful world, with its horizontal stripes of brown and white. And visible through moderate-size telescopes is its mysterious red spot. Orbiting the planet are at least sixteen moons, some worlds in their own right, larger than the planet Mercury.

Composite of photographs of Jupiter with its four Galilean moons, taken by cameras aboard Voyager 1. *Io is the smallest moon shown, Europa is in the center, Ganymede at the lower left and Callisto at the lower right.*

This planet and its moons have been examined ever since the invention of the telescope, but missions of two *Pioneer* and *Voyager* spacecraft gave us our first close-up views of the system.

The *Pioneer 10* and *11* spacecraft came near Jupiter in 1973 and 1974, and carried out an assortment of studies of the planet's atmosphere, magnetic field, radiation belts, and satellites. But it was the *Voyager* 1 and 2 spacecraft that unraveled many of the mysteries of the planet and its satellites in 1979.

For instance, an accidental photograph of the night side of Jupiter showed that it was surrounded by a faint ring. Huge lightning storms with bolts powerful enough to incinerate a city were detected and photographed as well. Ghostly aurora have been also discovered at the polar regions.

The true nature of the Great Red Spot is now known. It is a huge vortex of clouds—a hurricane larger than the earth—that was first observed three centuries ago. Smaller storms come and go, lasting a year or two, but the Great Red Spot spins on.

Then there are the satellites. One of them, Io, is one of the most fascinating objects in the Solar System. The *Voyagers* discovered that it was covered with active volcanoes: a dozen were viewed spewing forth material as the probes passed by. Much of the surface is molten sulfur, giving the world its beautiful yellow and orange colors.

Europa is another of Jupiter's moons. The *Voyagers* showed it to have a frozen and cracked crust, probably made of ice, a relatively thin crust covering a deep ocean of liquid water. This world may be a possible abode for life.

Io and Europa, as well as Callisto and Ganymede—the other major satellites of Jupiter—will be our landing points to study the planet. No person will ever visit Jupiter itself. There is no solid surface to walk on. Descending into the atmosphere, you would find it becoming thicker and hotter until you were immersed in a seething ocean of liquid hydrogen. The pressures and temperatures would be intolerable.

We expect to learn even more about the planet and its satellites when the *Galileo* space probe arrives there in the next few years. The main spacecraft will spend several months orbiting Jupiter, photographing it and its moons. As it arrives at Jupiter, it will release a probe to fall into the atmosphere of the planet. The probe will probably survive for only an hour but will transmit back to Earth a fantastic amount of data before the high temperatures and pressures of the planet cause it to fail.

SATURN

Most people know Saturn by its rings, even though we now know that other planets also have rings. They can be seen even through a small telescope. The rings have long been known to be made up of millions of tiny moons. But only when the spacecraft *Pioneer 11* and *Voyagers 1* and *2* arrived in 1979 and 1980 did we really appreciate this fact.

The rings had been subdivided by earthbound astronomers into five parts, labeled A through E. But the spacecraft showed us that there were hundreds, if not thousands, of ringlets, so many that they look like the grooves on a phonograph disk. Apparently the ring particles are herded together into individual rings by the gravitational influence of precisely placed moonlets. These are called "shepherding" moons.

"Spokes" in the rings were also noticed for the first time. These dark or light streaks run across the rings and appear to be radiating outward from the planet. They are believed to be caused by small, charged particles lifted above or below the rings by the planet's magnetic field.

The origin of the rings is still uncertain. Two theories are usually mentioned. One is that the rings represent leftover material that didn't form another moon when Saturn formed. The other theory says they are the pieces of a moon that did form but was pulled too close to the planet. Saturn's gravity ripped the moon apart, producing the debris we see today as rings.

The spacecraft also examined a number of the planet's major satellites. Titan, the most interesting, is the second largest moon in the Solar System, and the only one known to have an atmosphere. The atmosphere is predominantly nitrogen, like Earth's, but contains no oxygen, so you wouldn't be able to breathe it. Methane has an unusual role on Titan. It

apparently is abundant and at the right temperature to be in all three states—liquid, solid, and gas—just the way water is on Earth. If we ever explore Titan, we may have to send a submarine to cruise through its methane oceans.

The spacecraft also examined the planet itself. With a few notable exceptions, Saturn was found to be quite similar to Jupiter. For one thing, its markings are much fainter due to a thick smog that covers the planet. There are small spotlike vortices, but nothing like Jupiter's Great Red Spot. There is also a region near Saturn's equator where a huge thunderstorm is raging. The storm, about 40,000 miles (64,000 kilometers) across, is racing around the planet packing winds of up to 12,000 miles per hour (19,200 kilometers per hour). Nothing like it had ever been seen before on Saturn, or anywhere else, for that matter.

URANUS: ROLLING ON ITS SIDE

Until 1781, astronomers knew of only six planets: Mercury, Venus, Earth, Mars, Jupiter, and Saturn. But in that year, the German-born English astronomer William Herschel made a startling discovery. There was at least one more, Uranus.

For two centuries, we studied this planet from almost 1.8 billion miles (2.9 billion kilometers) away. With the best telescopes and equipment available, we had little to show for our efforts.

We knew that Uranus was a smaller version of Jupiter—4.1 times the diameter of Earth, but still one-third the diameter of the Solar System's giant. It was a gaseous planet, with some faint green horizontal stripes and five moons. If anything was unusual about Uranus, it was that it is tipped over nearly sideways on its axis, a greater tilt than any other planet. This was nearly the extent of our knowledge until two recent developments.

Saturn, photographed from Voyager 1 *on November 6, 1980, at a range of 5 million miles (8 million kilometers)*

Uranus, photographed by Voyager 2.
The moon Miranda is in the foreground.

In 1977, Uranus moved in front of a star. Astronomers eagerly study this kind of *eclipse* to learn about the planets. For instance, by timing an eclipse, they can measure the planet's diameter. Or by studying how the star's light fades out, they can determine the thickness of the planet's atmosphere and possibly its makeup. But this particular eclipse proved to be a surprise. Shortly before the eclipse, the starlight flickered several times. What this told astronomers was that Uranus was surrounded by rings! We now know that Uranus has at least nine rings.

New insight into the nature of Uranus occurred in January 1986, when *Voyager* reached the planet and gave us our first close-up views of Uranus and its rings.

What it found was a planet with fainter cloud markings than expected. It seems that Uranus is covered by a murky haze. One peculiar discovery concerned the planet's magnetic field. It is tilted at an angle of 60 degrees with respect to Uranus's axis of rotation. That is five times greater than the tilt of Earth's magnetic axis, the previous record holder.

The rings looked much as expected—narrow, dark, and sharply defined, with few surprises. Uranus's moons, however, were nearly all surprises. First of all, *Voyager* discovered ten new moons. Then it uncovered evidence of ice volcanoes on Oberon, the outermost satellite of Uranus. Ariel, with a diameter of 725 miles (1,160 kilometers) was thought to be too small to have much geologic activity. But it showed a network of branching, smooth-floored valleys. Miranda, the closest of the originally known moons, and half the size of Ariel, proved to be the weirdest of the moons. Its surface contains a huge cliff nearly 10 miles (16 kilometers) high, and large, rectangularly fractured areas with "racetrack patterns of ridges and grooves."

Scientists will continue to study the data sent back from *Voyager*'s encounter with Uranus for years. Undoubtedly there will be more surprises to come.

NEPTUNE: DOES IT HAVE RINGS, TOO?

While the discovery of Uranus was accidental, Neptune's was not. Two different people predicted the existence of this planet. This amazing event occurred nearly a century and a half ago, in 1845. Two young mathematicians, John Couch Adams in England and Urbain Leverrier in France, were attempting to solve a perplexing problem concerning the orbit of Uranus.

Uranus didn't quite follow the path predicted. Both these mathematicians decided that an unknown planet existed whose gravity was pulling on Uranus. Their work led to the discovery of Neptune in 1846.

This revolutionary way of discovering new planets or stars, by gravitationally detecting them before they are visually seen, is still used today. The only difference is that we have computers to carry out the calculations much faster and more accurately than Adams and Leverrier could.

The eighth planet appears to be quite similar to the seventh planet, only farther out. What little we know about it is due to telescopic observations from 2.8 billion miles (4.5 billion kilometers) off. *Voyager* 2 is scheduled to examine the planet, but not until 1989.

Eclipse studies of Neptune have been attempted. The results, however, are not clear. It appears that we will have to wait until 1989 to determine if the planet has rings like Jupiter, Saturn, and Uranus.

Neptune does have a pair of peculiar moons. The closest is Triton, a large satellite somewhere around 3,000 miles (4,800 kilometers) in diameter, which travels *backward* in orbit around Neptune—backward in that its orbiting direction is opposite to the way almost all of the Solar System, including the sun, orbits and spins. Recent studies of this moon indicate that tidal forces are causing it to slowly spiral inward toward the planet. In a billion years or so the same tidal forces will pull it apart, perhaps creating rings around Neptune.

The other moon, Nereid, has an extremely elongated orbit, coming to within 800,000 miles (1.3 million kilometers), of Neptune, then sailing outward to a distance of 6 million miles (9.6 million kilometers). Completing the full orbit requires a year. No other planet or moon in the Solar System follows such an eccentric orbit.

One more thing that *Voyager 2* will look for when it reaches Neptune is a possible third moon. Some astronomers have claimed there is evidence that one exists.

PLUTO: THE ICE PLANET

The last planet to be discovered was Pluto. Its existence was also predicted by the small remaining deviations in Uranus's

Artist's conception of a view of Neptune from the surface of its moon Triton

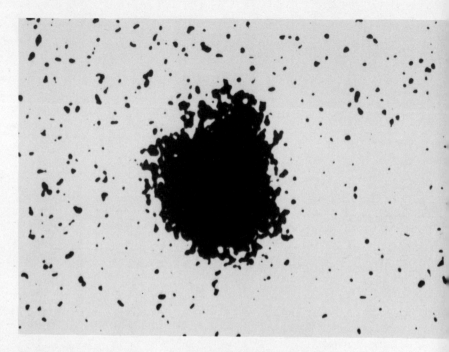

The dark spot in the middle of this negative is Pluto;
the arrow points to Charon, Pluto's one known moon.
In this picture, Charon looks like a bump on Pluto.

orbit. A number of astronomers thought a ninth planet responsible for these deviations, so they began a 20-year search for the missing planet. A young American astronomer named Clyde Tombaugh won this race in 1930. More than 60 years later, Pluto sails along in near darkness, keeping most of its secrets intact. And it is likely to do so for a considerable time in the future.

The surprising thing about the discovery of Pluto is that we now know it was a lucky accident. Pluto is much too small to have influenced Uranus, and the deviations were probably measurement errors anyway. Tombaugh just happened to be searching the right area of the sky with the right techniques at the right time—and suspected the existence of another planet, only for reasons that turned out to be wrong.

However Pluto was discovered, it is truly a mystery planet. The journey to Pluto is a long one, which would require decades to make with present spacecraft. *Voyager 2* spacecraft was not aimed toward Pluto. No other craft is likely to be sent in the near future.

One finding of note was made in 1978. Astronomers have photographed Pluto for more than 50 years, but even the best image has always been a tiny, blurred dot. However, upon close examination, the pictures often showed a "bump" on Pluto.

This bump proved to be a previously unknown moon, now called Charon. With this moon, scientists have finally been able to make an accurate measurement of Pluto's mass and density. It seems that the planet is largely ice.

Beginning in 1985, Charon started passing directly between the Sun and the planet, producing a series of eclipses on Pluto. These eclipses are being studied to learn more about the sizes and characteristics of the two bodies. Eclipses on Pluto are probably a lot rarer than on Earth. None had occurred since the discovery of the planet in 1930. When the current series of eclipses ends in a couple of years, another eclipse will not happen again until about 2109.

Though humans may someday wander this far from home, they are unlikely to find Pluto a desirable place to live. It is too cold, dark, and isolated from the rest of the Solar System.

CHAPTER 3
ROCKS
IN SPACE

*T*here is more to the sun's family than just nine planets and their moons. Floating through space are billions of mountains of ice and thousands of miniplanets. These are known to astronomers as *comets* and *asteroids*.

COMETS

Have you ever been lucky enough to see a comet? They are a magnificent sight. You often see them shortly after sunset or a bit before sunrise, silent feathers of light hanging in the sky. Some can be seen throughout the night. They seem to be motionless, yet they are hurtling through space at fantastic speeds.

Comets probably have been viewed with awe ever since humans began looking up at the heavens. But not until 400 years ago did we first begin to suspect their true nature.

For almost 2,000 years comets were believed to be a phenomenon of the earth's atmosphere. They were thought to be high-flying clouds, containing poisonous vapors that brought plague or ill fortune to humankind. They couldn't be far from the earth, for the Greek philosopher Aristotle had taught that nothing changed in the heavens beyond the moon's orbit. So they must be just high up in our atmosphere.

In 1577, the Danish astronomer Tycho Brahe (BRA-hee) laid these notions to rest. He calculated the distance to a bright comet that appeared in that year and showed that it was many millions of kilometers away—as far as the planets! It remained for Edmund Halley to prove that comets were law-abiding members of the sun's family, and not interstellar wanderers. He accomplished this by plotting the orbit of the Great Comet of 1680 (with Isaac Newton's help), showing that it indeed orbited the sun.

Since that time, astronomers have carefully plotted, drawn, and photographed hundreds of comets. Some have been seen to return every few decades. Others pass this way only once in a million years.

Today, we not only follow the orbits of comets, but we have sent spacecraft to intersect these orbits and to examine comets close up. So, what is a comet?

In truth, a comet is just a chunk of ice drifting through space. Billions of these ice chunks are orbiting at the farthest fringes of our Solar System. There is probably a spherical cloud of these comets out to a distance of about 1 *light-year* from the sun. A light-year is 6 trillion miles (9.5 trillion kilometers), the distance light travels in one year at the speed of 186,000 miles per second (300,000 kilometers per second). This has come to be known as the Oort comet cloud, after the Dutch astronomer Jan R. Oort, who in 1950 hypothesized its existence.

Comets are mountains of ice generally less than a few kilometers across—comparable to the size of large icebergs. The ice is mostly water ice (like the ice found on earth) and dry ice (frozen carbon dioxide). But there are also frozen ammonia and methane, as well as dust and grit mixed together. If we could put all of these mountains of ice together, we would probably produce an object a bit more massive than the earth.

Occasionally, one of these icebergs leaves the Oort comet cloud, perhaps because of a collision, or maybe due to the gravitational effects of a passing star. If it moves inward toward the sun, it has begun a journey that will require up to 6 million years! Initially, it might be moving at only a yard or two (a meter or two) per second. But as the comet falls inward, it will be accelerated by the solar gravity to a velocity that may exceed 600,000 miles per hour (1 million kilometers per hour).

The comet moves along too dim to be seen for the vast majority of its journey. Only for the last few years or so of its

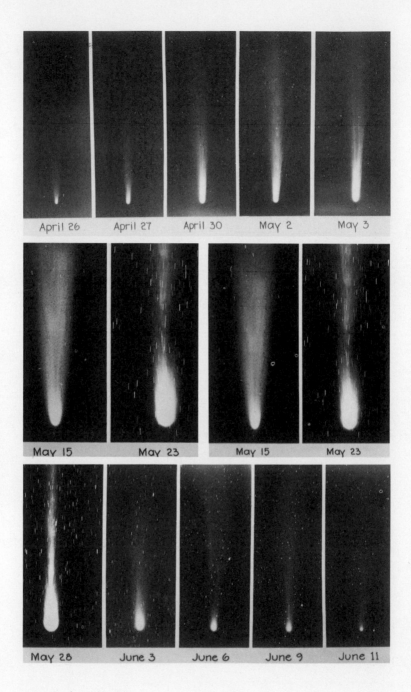

April 26 April 27 April 30 May 2 May 3

May 15 May 23 May 15 May 23

May 28 June 3 June 6 June 9 June 11

plunge does it finally enter the inner part of the solar system, crossing the orbits of Saturn and Jupiter and becoming visible to astronomers on Earth.

At first a comet appears like a fuzzy-looking star through the telescope. What we are observing is not actually the mountain of ice, called the *nucleus* (NOO-klee-us), but a surrounding cloud of material. Heat from the sun has vaporized some of the ices and produced an atmosphere called the coma (KO-ma). Eventually, enough material is vaporized so that it begins to stream away from the coma in a long tail (or tails). Strangely, this tail always points away from the sun, even when the comet itself is moving away from the sun. This was one of the first clues that there was such phenomenon as solar radiation and the *solar wind*. This is truly a wind of particles blowing away from the sun and pushing comet tails outward.

Most comets we see are passing by the sun for the first time in recorded history, if not for the first time altogether. Every now and then one of these comets passes close to one of the planets. Because of the pull of the planet's gravity, the comet's orbit is changed. Sometimes the comet is literally hurled out of the Solar System and lost permanently to interstellar space. On the other hand, the comet could be deflected into a smaller orbit that brings it back to the sun every few decades or so. What was once a long-period comet has become a short-period comet.

The most famous short-period comet is Comet Halley, with a period of about 76 years. How long a comet can continue to pass near the sun, losing material through evaporation, is not known. It varies from comet to comet, depending upon such things as the size of the comet, its exact composition, and how close it comes to the sun. But estimates show that a typical bright comet crossing the earth's orbit loses from 8 to 22 tons (7,000 to 20,000 kilograms) of material *per second.* This would allow a comet to pass close to the sun about a hundred times before it is mostly evaporated. So

Halley's comet in 1910

short-period comets are slowly disintegrating and being replaced by newly captured long-period comets.

A RAIN FROM SPACE

Have you ever noticed a "falling star"? What you might have seen is a piece of a comet. Although most of the lightweight gases that evaporate from a comet are swept from the Solar System by solar radiation pressure and the solar wind, the heavier sand and gravel-size particles are not. They remain in orbit around the sun, following the old comet's path. These are *meteoroids*. Most of the time, meteoroids sail peacefully through space. But occasionally a planet gets in the way. When this happens, they burn up in a fiery entry to the planet's atmosphere. This produces flashes of light known as *meteors*, more popularly referred to as shooting stars or falling stars.

Perhaps one time in a million the meteoroid may be as large as a golf ball. If so, it will survive its passage through our atmosphere and land on the ground. It then is known as a *meteorite*. Each year ten or twelve meteorite falls are reported around the world. Undoubtedly many more occur, but fall into the oceans. Occasionally houses and even people have been hit by meteorites. So far, however, we have been lucky. There are only a handful of cases in which someone was reported to have been killed by the fall of a meteorite. And none of these have occurred within the last 300 years.

Meteors burn up in the atmosphere every minute of the day. But now and then, the earth passes through a relatively fresh cometary orbit, producing many times the normal number of meteoroids. Then we see something called a meteor shower. These showers are seen every year on the same date, when the earth cuts across the cometary orbit. The table on page 60 lists a number of these meteor showers, along with the comet that produces them and the estimated meteor rates.

*A drawing of the meteor
shower of 1833*

Meteor Showers

Shower	Date	Comet	Rate
Quadrantid	Jan. 3	unknown	40-50 per hour
Lyrid	Apr. 21	1861 I	10-18 per hour
Eta Aquarid	May 4	Halley	10-40 per hour
Delta Aquarid	Jul. 30	unknown	10-35 per hour
Perseid	Aug. 12	1862 III	50-60 per hour
Draconid	Oct. 9	Giacobini-Zinner	20-30 per hour
Orionid	Oct. 20	Halley	25-35 per hour
Andromedid	Nov. 14	Biela	5-15 per hour
Leonid	Nov. 16	1866 I (Tempel)	5-20 per hour
Geminid	Dec. 13	unknown	50-80 per hour

Although comets have been studied by astronomers for centuries, only within the last two decades have we really come to understand these objects. For instance, although we had long suspected that comets must be made largely of water ice, water (H_2O)* had never been detected in a cometary spectrum. This is because the H_2O molecule is broken apart by sunlight as it evaporates (more properly, *sublimates*) from the nucleus of the comet.

In 1970, the Orbiting Astronomical Observatory, a robot spacecraft, detected hydrogen atoms (H) and hydroxyl ions (OH^-) in the ultraviolet spectrum of Comet Bennett. The hydroxyl ion is composed of one atom of oxygen (O) and one atom of hydrogen and has an overall negative charge. The intense sunlight experienced in space can break up the water molecule and also break up the hydrogen molecule (H_2) into hydrogen atoms. It also can ionize the hydrogen atoms into H^+ ions and free electrons.

It turns out that the head of a comet is surrounded by a huge cloud of hydrogen, which is not visible from the earth's surface. This is because most of its light is radiated in the

*Each element and molecule (more than one atom of an element) has its own symbol.

*The Leonid meteor shower photographed
from the Kitt Peak National Observatory
in Arizona on November 18, 1966*

ultraviolet wavelengths that do not penetrate the earth's atmosphere. But the discovery of H and OH in the hydrogen cloud strongly suggests that they are derived from H_2O. (We know that H_2O can be broken into H and OH in a chemical reaction.) While the head (composed of the nucleus and the coma) typically has a diameter of 63,000 miles (100,000 kilometers), the hydrogen cloud can be 31 million miles (50 million kilometers) across, one-third the distance from the earth to the sun.

Another example of the recent advances in cometry astronomy can be seen in the observations of the *SOLWIND* satellite. Launched in 1979, this satellite was designed to study the outer layers of the sun's atmosphere, where the solar wind begins. Much to astronomers' surprise, photographs showed undetected comets as they sped inward on a collision course with the sun. These comets had been missed by ground-based observations. Apparently, they were too small and dim to be visible until they were close to the glare of the sun.

Once in August 1979, three times in 1981, and once again in 1984, comets were seen by *SOLWIND* to hit the sun. A group of comets referred to as "sun grazers" had long been known to occasionally impact or nearly graze the sun as they passed. But suddenly, astronomers discovered that this family was much more numerous than had been thought and that more comets moved through the inner Solar System than previously believed.

COMET HALLEY— EVERY 76 YEARS

The most studied comet in history is Comet Halley, which has been observed at every passage by the sun since 239 B.C. The 1986 passage was the thirtieth that we can verify. Another indication of how astronomy has changed is seen by making comparisons in how Comet Halley was examined during its last two visits.

In 1910, the largest telescope in the world was the 60-inch (1.5-meter) reflector on Mount Wilson, in California. In 1986, the largest telescope was the 236-inch (6-meter) instrument on Mount Pastukhov in the Caucasus, in the Soviet Union. This telescope can gather sixteen times more light than the Mount Wilson instrument.

The idea of locating telescopes on a mountaintop to get above some of the atmosphere was revolutionary in 1910. In fact, the Mount Wilson telescope was one of the first such telescopes. In 1986, we had gone beyond mountaintops and even placed telescopes in orbit. This not only lifts the telescope above the obscuring effects of the atmosphere, it allows for nearly 24 hours of observing per day.

In 1910, the chief means available for studying a comet, beyond visual observation, was photography or spectroscopy. Spectroscopy—a technique for determining the chemical composition of an astronomical body by analyzing its light—

had shortly before been used to make the first chemical analysis of a comet. In 1986, photometers (to electronically measure light intensity), polarimeters (to measure the polarization, or orientation, of light waves), radio telescopes, infrared devices, and a variety of other instruments were trained on Comet Halley. So advanced have our techniques become that astronomers using a telescope equipped with a special device to brighten dim images were able to first detect Comet Halley 3.3 years before it reached *perihelion* (its closest approach to the sun), at a distance of 1 billion miles (1.6 billion kilometers). In 1910, the comet was first spotted only eight months before perihelion, at a distance of about 312 million miles (500 million kilometers).

COMETS UP CLOSE

The most spectacular example of how far we have come in astronomy is demonstrated by the international effort to study more than one comet by spacecraft. The planning for this effort involved more than a dozen nations and more than a decade of labor.

The first comet to be inspected by a spacecraft was Comet Giacobini-Zinner in September 1985. An American probe that had been monitoring the solar wind was redirected to pass close to this short-period comet. Although the spacecraft, renamed International Cometary Explorer (ICE), did not photograph the comet, it did return data on the composition, abundance, and release rate of cometary gases. These data were important for the careful positioning of the fleet of cometary probes on their way to a rendezvous six months later with Comet Halley.

That fleet included a European spacecraft named *Giotto,* two Japanese spacecraft called *Suisei* and *Sakigake,* and two Russian spacecraft named *Vega I* and *2.*

Giotto passed within 375 miles (600 kilometers) of Comet Halley, sending us the first close-up pictures of a comet's nucleus. Scientists were surprised to discover that the nucleus was much darker than expected—darker than coal. It also examined the dust and gases that surround the nucleus, using a *spectroscope* (to form a spectrum from the radiation), polarimeter, and three mass spectrometers (to analyze charged particles called ions).

Suisei was sent no closer than 125,000 miles (200,000 kilometers) from the nucleus to avoid the powerful "sand-blasting" that would occur to Giotto. Its instruments sent back photographs of the coma and studied the interaction of the solar wind with the comet. It's nearly identical twin, Saki-gake, viewed the comet from a distance of 4 million miles (6.4 million kilometers).

The Vega spacecraft were identical but launched two weeks apart. The first spacecraft was sent to within 5,550 miles (8,890 kilometers) of Comet Halley to make preliminary measurements of the coma and nucleus. It sent back narrow-angle and wide-angle photographs, as well as spectroscopic and polarization measurements. It also photographed the nucleus with an infrared camera. Based upon this probe's data, Vega 2's path was adjusted to pass slightly closer to the comet (5,020 miles or 8,030 kilometers), sending back higher-resolution photos and information from a different section of the comet's coma.

In one great leap, our knowledge of comets has increased more than tenfold. Although it was the space probes that dominated the headlines, much of the puzzle's details were gathered by other sources. A worldwide organization of observers known as International Halley Watch amassed huge amounts of information on the comet. It will be a number of years before we finish reaping the benefits of this one harvest.

ASTEROIDS: FLYING MOUNTAINS

A less spectacular minor member of the sun's family is the group of objects known as asteroids, or minor planets.

These bodies have been observed by astronomers ever since in 1801 Giuseppe Piazzi discovered the asteroid that became known as Ceres. Although it was at first thought that Piazzi had located the long-sought "missing planet" be-tween the orbits of Mars and Jupiter, it soon became appar-ent that Ceres was not the only object orbiting the Sun at this distance. Within a decade, three more asteroids were found between Mars and Jupiter. The largest asteroid, Ceres, is just under 600 miles (1,000 kilometers) across. Another thirty are larger than 125 miles (200 kilometers) in diameter. But most are just a few miles across or smaller.

More than three thousand asteroids have been studied closely enough to have their orbits determined. These have been named, numbered, and cataloged. Estimates are that probably a hundred thousand such bodies could be spotted by earth-based telescopes, if we were to conduct a thorough search. This is a large number of objects, but they still don't amount to much. If they were all collected together, their mass wouldn't equal one-tenth the mass of our moon.

The most likely explanation for the origin of the asteroids is that they represent unused bricks from the construction of our Solar System. About 4.6 billion years ago, when the sun formed, quite a bit of material was left over, most of it orbiting the sun in a number of rings. Gradually each one of these rings collected to form a planet. However, the ring just inside the orbit of Jupiter found it difficult to form a planet. Every time it began to collect into a single body, the huge planet Jupiter swept by, its strong gravitational forces stirring up the collecting material and keeping it from forming a single object. Instead, many miniplanets probably formed. These collided with one another over the eons, producing thousands of fragments. These fragments are the asteroids we see today.

ARE ASTEROIDS A HAZARD?

In the early 1970s, when spacecraft were being prepared to be sent to the outer planets, the asteroid belt was a major concern. Would a spacecraft be likely to encounter more than a few routine impacts from interplanetary micrometeoroids (sand-size particles in space)? Although they travel at several thousands of miles per hour, micrometeoroids do not normally carry enough energy to damage a spacecraft. However, something the size of a marble, or larger, could seriously damage or destroy a spacecraft.

Scientists were greatly relieved when *Pioneer 10* and *11* passed through the asteroid belt in 1971, and *Voyagers 1* and *2* made the journey in 1974. None of the spacecraft was hit by anything large enough to injure them. Although a lot of large chunks of material are in the belt, there is not enough small debris to create a significant hazard.

It has long been known that most asteroids show regular variations in brightness. This is caused by the rotation of the objects around their axes. Periods of rotation range from 2.5 to 85 hours, with the large asteroids having a typical period of about 8 hours. By studying how the light brightens and dims, astronomers have been able to deduce the shape and dimensions of many asteroids. For although it is true that the largest asteroids are fairly spherical, most are so small that the force of their own gravity is not enough to shape them into a sphere. One example is Eros, whose brightness varies by a factor of five in a period of 5.3 hours. From this and other data we can deduce that it is brick shaped, with dimensions of 16 miles by 5 miles by 5 miles (25 kilometers by 8 kilometers by 8 kilometers), and spinning about its shortest axis.

Although we have never photographed the surface of an asteroid, we have photographed the surfaces of two small bodies of asteroidal mass and size—Phobos (diameter: 17 miles or 27 kilometers) and Deimos (diameter: 9 miles or 15 kilometers), the satellites of Mars. It is likely that these moons are asteroids captured by Mars. *Viking* spacecraft photographs from 1976 show them as being extremely dark bodies, irregular in shape, and heavily cratered. NASA has announced that it hopes to send the Galileo *Jupiter* probe on a path that will take it to within 6,300 miles (10,000 kilometers) of one of the larger asteroids.

One tool recently brought to bear on the problem of asteroids is the infrared spectrometer, a device that records and analyzes the infrared radiation reflected by an asteroid. From it, we can get an idea of the composition of the asteroids. In general, there are three types of asteroids: carbonaceous, composed mostly of carbon; silicaceous, composed mostly of the element silicon; and metallic, composed mostly of metals such as iron and nickel.

Recently radar waves have been bounced off of several asteroids in an attempt to learn more about these objects. In this way astronomers have discovered that their surfaces are probably covered with a dusty layer similar to that on our moon.

Occasionally asteroids pass in front of distant stars, producing eclipses. These events provide one way by which asteroidal diameters can be determined. But since 1978, scientists have been studying asteroid eclipses for another reason. In that year, a rather interesting eclipse was pro-

Phobos, one of the two Martian moons, as photographed by the orbiter of Viking 1 *in February 1977*

duced by the minor planet 532 Herculina. After the background star returned to view from behind the asteroid, there was a brief secondary eclipse, which might signify the existence of a small moon orbiting Herculina. Another group of scientists has put forth the name of 146 Lucina as a second asteroid that has shown a similar peculiar eclipse. Although many astronomers maintain that the evidence is too insubstantial to confirm the existence of asteroidal moons, there is a renewed interest in such eclipses.

HAVE ASTEROIDS HIT THE EARTH?

Perhaps the most exciting and controversial theory concerning asteroids has to do with their striking the Earth. Scientists have long known that such objects do occasionally hit our planet. Though most asteroids are found in nearly circular orbits between Mars and Jupiter, some follow elliptical paths that cut across the Earth's orbit. These asteroids are called *Apollo asteroids,* after the first such object discovered.

About fifty Apollo asteroids are known, but twenty times that number may exist that have diameters larger than 0.6 mile (1 kilometer). Calculations have been made concerning the probability of these objects hitting the earth.

It appears that an asteroid 6 miles (10 kilometers) in diameter will impact the earth every 100 million years or so. In doing so, it will blast out a crater 130 miles (200 kilometers) across and throw a tremendous amount of dust into the atmosphere. This dust will require years to drift slowly down out of the upper atmosphere. In the meantime, the amount of light reaching the earth's surface will be significantly reduced. Studies indicate that this would kill much of the plant life as well as temporarily reduce the earth's temperature. This would combine to starve or otherwise kill off most of the animal kingdom. There would be a tremendous extinction of life on this planet.

Geologists know that during the 570 million years of recorded fossil history of advanced life forms, there have been a number of large and widespread biological extinctions. The most recent of these was approximately 65 million years ago when the dinosaurs (and a lot of other species) died out. A variety of theories have been put forward to explain this event. In 1979, Luis and Walter Alvarez of the University of California at Berkeley added one more.

They discovered that in a number of places around the globe, 65-million-year-old rocks show an enrichment of the element iridium. This element is relatively rare on earth but somewhat plentiful in meteorites and asteroids. Their hypothesis is that we were hit by an asteroid at that time. This resulted in a temporary change in climate and a permanent extinction of a huge number of species.

Other scientists have recently shown that rocks from this same period have a higher than normal amount of ash and smoke particles in them. This may be further evidence of a powerful impact which ignited huge forest fires on a global scale.

The Alvarezes's theory has not gone unchallenged, but it has found a number of advocates. It also has opened a number of people's eyes to the potential problems following such an impact—or, for that matter, a nuclear war. The end result is renewed interest in the detection of Apollo asteroids and the prediction of their trajectories.

CHAPTER 4
STELLAR EVOLUTION: THE BIRTH OF STARS

One November evening in 1572, the great Danish astronomer Tycho Brahe went for a walk and happened to look up at the sky. He was astounded to see a bright star where he had not seen one before. He was so surprised that he called to his servants to confirm that there really was a "new" star in the sky. The ancients had believed that stars always had been and always would be. This belief is understandable since casual examination of the sky from time to time does not reveal any changes.

What Tycho discovered was called a *nova,* which means "new star." Today we know that it really wasn't a *new* star, but rather a star dying a fiery *death.* A study of these stars is only part of the story of how stars are born, how they live out their lives, and how they die.

Up until the last several decades, astronomers believed that all stars lived and died in pretty much the same way. Today we know this is not true. New information gained by tools such as radio telescopes, infrared satellites, and X-ray satellites have revealed clues about stellar life and death that now make astronomers believe that the life, and particularly the death, of stars is different for different types of stars.

The story of the life cycle of the star includes "chapters" on such stellar objects as planetary nebulas, white dwarfs, neutron stars, pulsars, supernova remnants, and black holes. The story of the life cycle of the star has been one of the major revolutions in astronomy. Most people have heard of pulsars and black holes, but they have provided astronomers with the key notes to the conclusion of the exciting revolution of thought about stellar evolution that began in the early 1900s.

HOW TO STUDY THE LIFE OF A STAR

Compared with the short life span of a human being, the life of a star continues for a very long time—perhaps billions of years. We cannot hope to see the whole life history of a star from birth to death in one human lifetime. All we can do is study clues from a huge number of normal and unusual objects in the sky and try to put together a complete, reasonable story.

To do this we need to know many things about stars—for example: How far away are stars? How bright are the stars? How hot are they? What are stars made of? How much matter is in a star? How big are they?

Until astronomers could answer these questions, the life story of stars could not be completed. Our story of stellar evolution starts by exploring these fundamental questions.

HOW FAR, HOW BRIGHT?

We measure the distances to stars using a method called *parallax*. Hold one of your fingers out at arm's length and close one eye. Line the finger up with a spot on the wall. Now open the closed eye and close the other. Then alternate eyes. Your finger will appear to jump back and forth. This is an example of parallax. The closer you bring your finger to your face, the bigger this parallax displacement will be.

Since the time of the pyramids, surveyors have used a slightly more sophisticated version of this technique to measure distances. Astronomers, learning from the surveyors, decided that parallax could be used to measure distances in the heavens. As the earth moves in its orbit around the sun, an observer on earth using a telescope will see the close stars appear to jump back and forth in the same way as your finger appeared to jump back and forth. From a photographic plate the amount or angle of displacement can be more easily

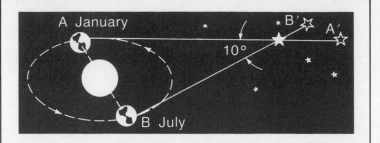

To measure the parallax shift of a star, astronomers photograph the star from one point in the earth's orbit around the sun, then six months later photograph the star from the opposite side of the orbit. In the example here, a parallax shift of 10 degrees can be measured as the star seems to move from position A′ to B′ as the observer moves from A to B.

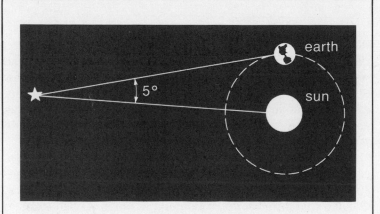

The parallax angle is half the angle of parallax shift—in this case, 5 degrees.

measured. The smaller the angle, the farther away is the star. Using this method is difficult, but about ten thousand stars have had their distances measured in this way.

The closest star we know of today is Proxima Centauri, which is part of the triple star system called Alpha Centauri and only 4.3 light-years away. This star is said to have a parallax angle of only 0.76 second of arc, a *very* small angle. (You are probably familiar with degrees of angular measurement—a circle has 360 degrees. Each degree can be further divided into 60 minutes, and each minute into 60 seconds. To avoid confusion with units of time or temperature, reference is made to degrees of arc, minutes of arc, and seconds of arc.) To get an idea of how small this is, hold your finger out at arms length. The angle covered or subtended by the width of your finger at your eye is about two degrees. Since there are 3,600 seconds in one degree of arc, the width of your finger subtends an angle of 7,200 seconds of arc. If you could slice your finger lengthwise into 7,200 very thin slices (not that you would want to), each slice would still subtend a parallax angle larger than the parallax of Proxima Centauri!

We express the brightness of a star on a scale of *apparent magnitudes.* The brightest stars have the smallest magnitudes (+1, +2, etc.) or even zero or negative numbers. For example, the brightest visible star, Sirius, has an apparent magnitude of –1.4. We use photographs or a modern device called a photometer—which measures the intensity of light—to measure the brightnesses of stars. The brightnesses of thousands of stars have been measured. (Amateur astronomers have contributed greatly to the measurement of stellar brightness through an organization called the American Association of Variable Star Observers.)

Since stars are at different distances from earth, astronomers have adopted a scale of *absolute magnitudes* in order to compare the true luminosities, or the absolute brightness, of stars. They do this by comparing the brightnesses of stars as if all of them were placed 32.6 light-years from the earth. For example, the sun has an *apparent* magnitude of −26.5. But if it were 32.6 light-years away, it would have an *absolute* magnitude of +4.8. It would be so dim that you would have to have good eyesight and a very dark sky to see it.

WHAT ARE STARS MADE OF?

Astronomers attach a device called a *spectrograph* to telescopes. This instrument takes the starlight and spreads it into a *spectrum* of colors. Raindrops do the same thing for the sun, and we see the sun's spectrum as a rainbow. But if you look closely at the sun's spectrum, or the *spectra* (plural of spectrum) of other stars, you will see that they are crossed with dark lines. These lines are the "fingerprints" of different chemical elements. We find that stars like the sun are made mostly of hydrogen (about 75 percent) and helium (about 22 percent), with only tiny amounts of all the rest of the elements put together.

Also, by studying the brightest part of the spectrum, astronomers can tell the temperature of a star. The hottest stars are blue—the blue part of the spectrum is most intense. Cool stars are red—in cool stars the red part of the spectrum is strongest.

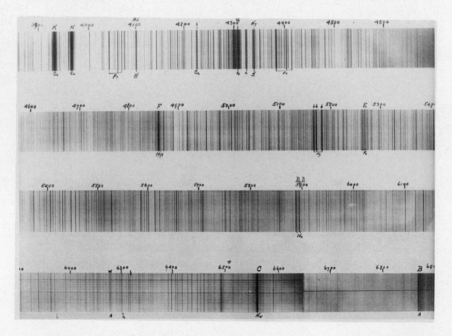

The spectrum of the sun

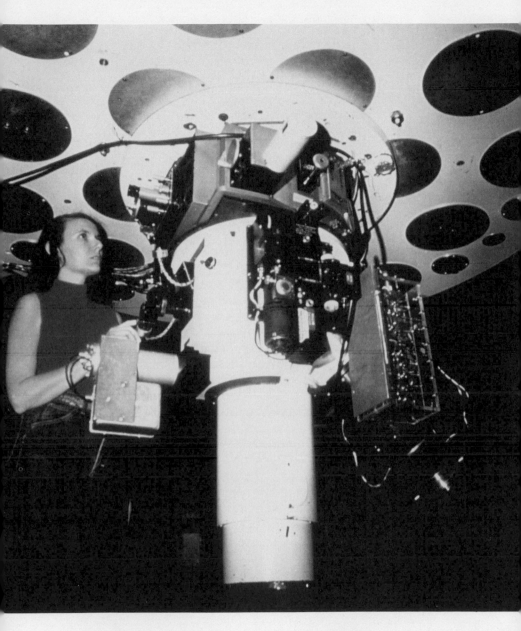

An astronomer examines a spectrograph attached to a telescope at the Kitt Peak Observatory.

Our sun looks yellow because it is a star of medium temperature (about 11,000 degrees Fahrenheit, or 6,000 degrees Celsius); the sequence of colors in the spectrum is red, orange, yellow, green, blue, and violet. Yellow falls between hot blue and cool red.

HOW MUCH AND HOW BIG?

One technique used to study the sizes and masses of stars uses *binary stars,* stars that orbit each other. Most stars belong to such binary systems. The sun seems to be an exception, but a few astronomers believe that the sun just might have a distant companion, too. They call this undiscovered star Nemesis. The evidence for its existence is controversial; most astronomers do not believe there is such a star.

If we happen to see one of these binary stars so their orbit is just edge on, each star will pass in front of the other, periodically causing two eclipses. By measuring the duration of the eclipse and by knowing how fast the stars are moving, astronomers can calculate the diameter of the stars.

What have we found? Some stars are about the size of the sun; others are very small, no bigger than the earth. These are called white dwarf stars. On the other hand, some red stars are truly giant stars. The bright red star Aldebaran (known as "the eye of the bull") in the constellation Taurus is fifty times larger than the sun. Put in the middle of the Solar System, it would cover the orbit of Mercury. Some stars are even larger. The diameter of Betelgeuse, in the constellation Orion ("the hunter") is over five hundred times the sun's diameter. If Betelgeuse were in the middle of our Solar System, it would extend to the orbit of Jupiter! These are called red supergiant stars.

An ordinary telescope just shows stars as bright spots of light. Speckle interferometry (see Chapter 1) has been used to actually get pictures that show the disk of a star. One of the first stars to be studied this way was Betelgeuse. The results showed that our indirect measurements were correct, and even showed spots like those on our own sun.

Binary stars can also be used to "weigh" stars. The

earth goes around the sun at a distance of 93 million miles (150 million kilometers). It does so, in one year, because the mass of the sun produces a gravity tug. If we find other stars that go around each other at the same distance from each other, and do so in one year, we know that their combined mass equals that of the earth and the sun. Since the earth is very light compared to the sun, we say the combined mass is "one solar mass." If they go around each other faster (or closer), they contain more mass, which results in stronger gravitational tugging. The study of binary stars reveals stars with as little as 0.04 solar mass and as much as 40 solar masses.

THE GRAND PATTERN OF STARS

Two astronomers making a graph of the stars' absolute magnitudes and temperatures independently discovered an interesting pattern. In the early part of this century, astronomers had measured a number of star brightnesses, distances, and temperatures. E. Hertzsprung of Holland and H. R. Russell of the United States were the first to make a graph of temperatures and absolute magnitudes. Their graphs, now called Hertzsprung-Russell (or H-R) diagrams, provided the first important clue to the lives of stars. Most of the hot stars are luminous, and most of the cool stars are dim. But there were a few hot dim stars (the white dwarfs) and a number of high-luminosity cool stars (the red supergiants) like Betelgeuse. The story of star life and death—stellar evolution—has to account for all of these types of stars.

HOW ARE STARS BORN?

The story of star life has to start with star birth. But the question can be asked: "From what are stars born?"

Astronomers have known for years that there are huge clouds of gas between the stars called *nebulas* (NEB-you-las), which are made of the same elements as the stars— mostly hydrogen and helium and in similar proportions. This is an important clue.

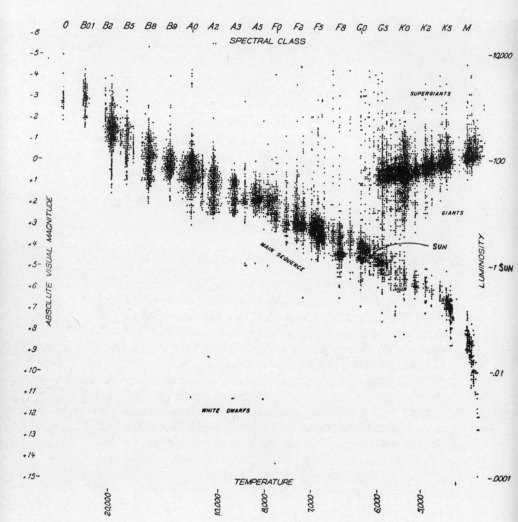

The Hertzprung-Russell diagram plots absolute magnitude or luminosity against temperature or spectral type for stars. Most stars lie along the main sequence. Stars on their way toward "extinction" leave the main sequence. These include the red giants and supergiants as well as the white dwarfs, which are what's left of stars that are almost burnt out.

The Dumbbell Nebula, a planetary nebula in the constellation Vulpecula

It is a law of gas behavior that a contracting (compressed) gas will heat up. You probably have noticed that the air in a bicycle tire gets hot as it is pumped up to the right pressure. If a nebula were to start contracting, its gravitational potential energy would be changed to heat energy. By the time the nebula, starting at thousands of times larger than our own Solar System, were to shrink to a size just big enough to include the earth's orbit, the center of the gas cloud would reach a temperature of 2 million degrees Fahrenheit (1.1 million degrees Celsius). It is now glowing from the heat.

As the volume continues to decrease the temperature rises higher and higher. A few million years after the nebula starts to contract, the temperature of the center reaches 18 million degrees Fahrenheit (10 million degrees Celsius). At this point the pressure and temperature are high enough to start what astronomers call the proton-proton chain. This is a nuclear reaction in which four hydrogen nuclei (protons) merge or fuse together to form helium. In doing this, large amounts of energy are given off. A star is born!

A gas tends to dissipate. Notice how the aroma of a cologne or perfume rapidly spreads throughout a room. In a stable nebula there is a balance between the tendency to dissipate and the tendency to contract. What upset this balance and started the contraction that led to a star birth? Astronomers believe that nebular collapses are triggered by shock waves arising from two sources. One source is the high-speed waves of compressed gas (shock waves) ejected by supernovas, the explosions of massive stars. The other source is the Lin density waves (named for the Chinese astronomer who first studied them) that travel through the gas and dust of galaxies. Their origin is not yet understood.

The evidence for this concept comes from studies by the famous Harvard astronomer Bart Bok of what are called Bok

*The Horsehead Nebula
in the constellation Orion*

Globules—small dark regions of condensed gas clouds on their way to becoming stars.

HOW LONG DO STARS LIVE?

We now believe that the star goes through a protected childhood. The American astronomer G. Herbig and the Mexican astronomer G. Haro have investigated what are now called Herbig-Haro objects. Astronomers are now convinced that these are the cocoons or shells of gas and dust surrounding a recently born star. Infrared satellite measurements of these objects detect the presence of young, unstable stars inside Herbig-Haro objects.

After a star is born (perhaps in just a few years), the cocoon is pushed away by the solar wind and the radiation pressure and the star reveals itself as a normal star to our eyes.

Stars that start out with more raw materials to begin with are much more wasteful of their fuel. A star like the sun will live for about 10 billion years. But if a star starts out with ten times the raw material of the sun, it will only live a few million years. Yet we see stars in the sky like the sun and stars ten times as massive. This must mean that stars are being born all the time.

Is that what Tycho saw, a star being born? No, we think stars are born rather quietly, but some die in a grand explosion. This is the story of the next chapter.

CHAPTER 5
STELLAR EVOLUTION: DYING STARS

Astronomers now know that stars produce energy by fusing hydrogen nuclei to produce heavier elements. (The *nucleus,* or core, of a hydrogen atom is a *subatomic particle*—a proton.) In the process, a small percentage of matter is converted directly into energy. The amount of energy released is given by Einstein's famous equation $E = mc^2$, where E is the energy, m is the mass, and c is the speed of light. Since c is such a big number, even a little matter directly converted to energy produces a huge amount of energy.

For example, converting *all* the matter in an ordinary baseball (about 1 pound or 500 grams) into energy would produce enough energy to keep a 100-watt light bulb burning for *10 million years!* Such energy is difficult to produce on earth, but stars do it all the time.

Yet even in stars, the fuel eventually must run out and the stars die, and astronomers in the last two decades have discovered that stars die in at least several different ways. A star similar to our sun dies a gentle death and leaves behind a white dwarf star. Massive stars die violent deaths, their end coming with the violent explosion called a supernova. These stars leave behind exotic beasts in the cosmic zoo, possibly a compact star called a neutron star or the strangest beast of all, a very small, very dense core which collapses to form a black hole.

DEATH OF THE SUN

Stars like the sun use up their hydrogen fuel at a very leisurely rate. Each *second* our sun changes 600 *million* tons of hydrogen into 595.5 million tons of helium.* This means that about 4.5 million tons of matter are converted directly into energy each second. To give you an idea of how much matter that is, here's an analogy: A typical car weighs about 1.5 tons, so 4 million tons is about 2.6 million cars, about the number of cars in New York City. (Their conversion into energy would help New York City's parking problem, wouldn't it?)

As large as this number is, there is still enough fuel in the sun to last another 5 *billion* years. But what happens when the fuel in the core of the sun runs out? Keep in mind that only in the core of the sun are the temperatures and pressures high enough to fuse hydrogen nuclei to produce helium and energy.

After about 10 percent of the hydrogen in the sun has been converted to helium, the sun will begin to expand and cool very gradually. Any observers on earth 5 billion years from now would probably not notice any changes in the sun's size or temperature—or in the earth's temperature—in their lifetime. After thousands of years the earth will start to get hotter; the oceans will boil, and the air will be lost to space. Life as we know it will be exterminated. Humankind will have had to migrate to other worlds in order to survive.

What will happen next? The sun will not become a supernova: our sun is not massive enough to become a supernova. A distant observer would see our sun become a *red giant*. Its central temperature will then be about 180 million degrees Fahrenheit (100 million degrees Celsius) and it will begin to fuse helium nuclei to release energy and form carbon nuclei. After years the outer atmosphere of the sun will be blown off as a glowing shell of gas.

Astronomers have discovered thousands of these gas shells, called planetary nebulas. In the center of each such planetary nebula is a small, hot star—a *white dwarf*. This is the final fate of the sun. There is no more nuclear fuel in its core that it can burn, and with no more fuel to burn, the star

*Metric units aren't given because the difference between a ton and a metric ton is minimal. If you wish to convert, 1 ton = 0.9 metric ton.

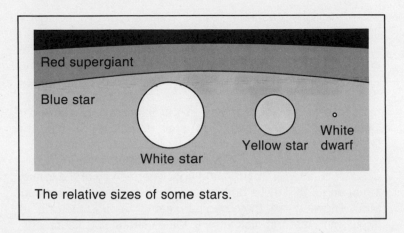

Red supergiant

Blue star

White star

Yellow star

White dwarf

The relative sizes of some stars.

gently contracts until it becomes earth size. The intense pressure packs the atomic parts so close together that one teaspoon of the white dwarf weighs about 5 tons (5,000 kilograms)! This is like compressing three automobiles down into the bowl of an ordinary teaspoon!

SOME STARS DIE
IN A GRAND WAY

Remember the bright star that Tycho saw? We now know it was a *supernova*. That particular star is now known as Tycho's supernova. Scientists believe that these are really the death explosions of stars much more massive than the sun. These energetic events don't happen very often. Only once in about every 50 to 150 years do astronomers find a supernova in any one galaxy. The last one seen in our own galaxy was in 1604. (We are past due for one in our Milky Way galaxy. Perhaps some have occurred but were hidden by local gas and dust clouds.)

What causes these explosions, and what happens to the star after it explodes? One of the best-studied supernovas was first spotted by Chinese astronomers in A.D. 1054. This is when the light reached the earth. The event producing the light actually happened thousands of years before. On the morning of July 4, 1054 A.D. a very bright star appeared in the constellation Taurus. For weeks it was the brightest star in the sky, shining so brightly as to be visible during the day. Years later, the famous French comet hunter Messier noticed a large cloud of gas in the same place where the Chinese had spotted this bright star. He called the cloud the Crab Nebula because he thought it looked like a crab.

During this century, Edwin Hubble and others found the Crab Nebula to be about 4,000 light-years away and expanding at about 900 miles per second (1,450 kilometers per second). Knowing this, they then calculated the time the original explosion was first visible. The date, about 900 years ago, coincided with records of the Chinese observation of the supernova.

During the 1930s, the American astronomers Fritz Zwicky and Walter Baade, predicted that the colossal explosion of a supernova would leave behind a large ball of neutrons, the tiny neutral particles found in the nuclei of all atoms except hydrogen. The force of the explosion would drive the protons and electrons in atoms together to make neutrons, and these, combined with neutrons normally found in atoms,* would be packed into a dense ball only a few *miles* (or *kilometers*) across. A teaspoon of a *neutron star* is estimated to weigh 40 million tons. To return to our car analogy, this would be equivalent to packing *all* the cars in the United States into one spoonful. Back in the 1930s, most people believed that we would never see neutron stars. After all, could you hope to see a star only the size of a small city from thousands of light-years away? But as has happened so often in astronomy, new tools changed everything.

STARS THAT TICK

During the 1960s Jocelyn Bell, a young graduate student at Cambridge University in England, was working with Anthony

---

*Since hydrogen is the most abundant element, most of the neutrons would be newly formed.

The Crab Nebula in the constellation Taurus

Hewish using a very large but simple radio telescope. This telescope, called the Four Acre Array, looks like a large field of posts and wires. Hewish was interested in how radio signals are changed as they pass through the thin matter between the stars. In late November 1967, Bell noted that some radio signals showed an extremely regular pattern occurring every 1.3 seconds (1.33728 seconds, to be exact). This was odd. Most radio signals from space do not pulse this quckly, and no quartz watch could keep better time.

At first, Bell and Hewish thought the pulse might be signals from an alien civilization, but the discovery of other, similar radio sources meant the sources must be natural objects. To date, more than five hundred of these objects, known as

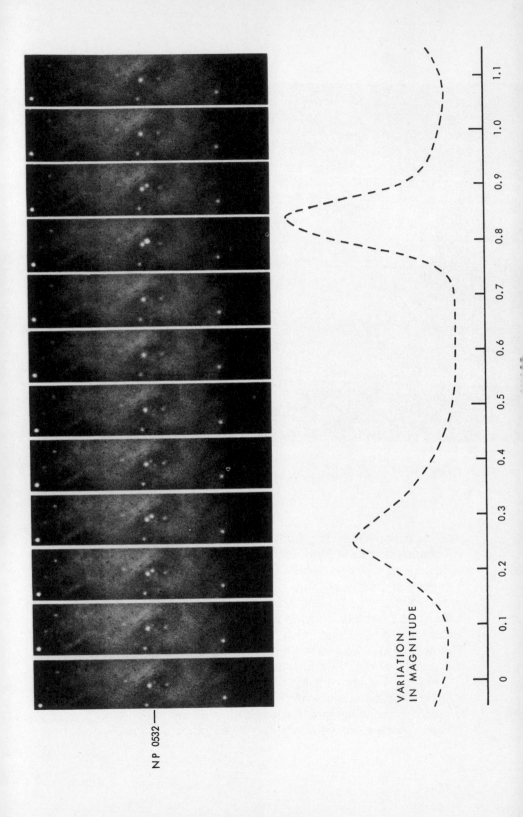

NP 0532

VARIATION IN MAGNITUDE

0   0.1   0.2   0.3   0.4   0.5   0.6   0.7   0.8   0.9   1.0   1.1

pulsars, have been identified. One has even been discovered in the middle of the Crab Nebula, ticking about thirty times each second. What is a pulsar and how does it work?

Just as ice skaters will spin faster when they pull in their outstretched arms, so will a large, slowly spinning star speed up if it collapses. At the same time the star's magnetic fields will get much stronger.

Strong magnetic fields attached to a rapidly spinning sphere (neutron star) will cause protons and electrons on the surface to spiral around and emit radio waves in a beam. As the neutron star spins, this beam sweeps over an observer (if he is in the right direction) just like the light from a light house. We now believe that a pulsar is a rapidly spinning neutron star, and it is heard or seen only because the observer is in the right place to "see" the beam sweep by. Astronomers discovered the Zwicky-Baade neutron stars without really looking for them.

Recently several astronomers detected visible light coming from the pulsar neutron star at the center of the Crab Nebula. The light "turns on and off" at the same frequency as the radio signals emitted from the star. For the first time ever we have "seen" the star the Chinese saw explode over 900 years ago.

OTHER PULSAR DISCOVERIES

More recently astronomers have discovered pulsars that flash thousands of times per second, called millisecond pulsars. These stars emit intense bursts of radiation. The energy from these "flashers," as they are known, is enormous.

The sequence of photos shows the visible-light variation of the pulsar at the center of the Crab Nebula. The pulsar's light has a regular cycle of thirty times per second. The graph shows the variation in magnitude over one cycle.

According to one current speculation, flashers probably are located in the gas remains of a supernova in a nearby galaxy. If this is so, the energy must be a hundred thousand times the energy of similar objects in our own galaxy. Another idea is that some neutron stars are in orbit with supergiant stars and that material from the giant star falls onto the neutron star and is sent into pulses by the rotating beams. These are mysteries still to be investigated.

BLACK HOLES

What happens if a really massive star, thirty to forty times the mass of the sun, explodes at the end of its life? What if it leaves behind a small, dense ball of matter with a gravitational field strong enough to prevent even light from escaping the star?

As early as 1796, the French mathematician Pierre LaPlace thought of light as tiny corpuscles, like little marbles. He realized that they would be unable to escape from the surface of supermassive bodies. He called these bodies *corps obscurs,* meaning "obscure bodies." There was no way to test his idea, and eventually it disappeared from scientific writing.

After Einstein's new theory of gravitation appeared in the early 1900s, the German physicist Karl Schwarzschild calculated what *space* would be shaped like around a point mass. His conclusion was that the shape of space would be so sharply curved that light would not be able to get out from this deeply curved "gravity well." In recent years the physicist John Wheeler invented the name *black hole* for such an object.

Then in 1939, the physicist J. Robert Oppenheimer showed that a massive star could collapse and form a black hole. These might be real objects, not just the result of hypothetical and mathematical games such as those that LaPlace and Schwarzschild had been playing.

There is a striking parallel between the discovery of neutron stars and that of black holes. Both had been hypothesized before the tools were developed to discover them.

Although the direct observation of a black hole is impossible because no electromagnetic radiation (including light)

*Astronomers think the bright star near the center
of the photograph is the companion of Cygnus X-1,
the first suspected black hole.*

could escape, they do have gravitational effects on objects around them.

One suggestion was that if one star in a binary pair becomes a supernova and part of it collapses to form a region of sharply curved space—a black hole—it might still affect its companion star. The black hole could pull matter away from its companion, and as this gas was drawn into the hole, friction would heat the matter to such high temperatures that energy would be released.

The new technology of X-ray satellites made possible the first discovery of black holes.

On December 12, 1970, the satellite *Uhuru* was launched from the Kenya coast. (It was the Kenyan Independence Day, and *Uhuru* in Swahili means "freedom.") This satellite was designed to pinpoint strong X-ray sources better than we could ever do before. One source detected was in the summer constellation Cygnus, near the giant star HDE 226868. Stars like this are normal stars that are up to ten times more massive than the sun, and are *not* known to produce X-rays.

What was the source of the X-rays? Examination of the spectrum of HDE 226868 led scientists to the conclusion that HDE 226868 is orbiting another object every 5.6 days. The other object had to be very massive, and yet it is invisible. Could the object be a black hole?

Today we believe that this star and the (possible) black hole are in a cosmic dance. Gas drawn into the black hole is pulled into a donut-shaped disk around the black hole. Gas spirals in, faster and faster, and finally is pulled into the black hole. Recently, William Kaufmann has used supercomputers to show that bubbles of gas will well up out of the donut, producing intense X-rays. Most astronomers agree that we finally may be "seeing" a black hole after all. This has been named Cygnus X-1.

Astronomers now believe they have an even better black hole candidate in an object known as LMC X-3, in a nearby galaxy called the Large Magellanic Cloud. LMC X-3 appears to be an invisible X-ray source with ten times the mass of the sun. Anything that massive should be visible unless it is a black hole.

OTHER BLACK HOLES

The collapse of a giant dying star may not be the only way to produce black holes. Giant black holes may have formed in baby galaxies billions of years ago. Stephen Hawking, a British astrophysicist, thinks the early universe may have produced tiny black holes (as massive as a mountain) that would "evaporate" in a burst of energy about 15 billion years after formation. This is about the current age of the universe. If so, we should see these bursting right now. So far, astronomers are looking, but without success.

CHAPTER 6
DISCOVERING GALAXIES

*A*ncient people were fascinated by the sky, with its count-less and unreachable stars. The Milky Way held a partic-ular fascination. Each culture impressed its own values on this shimmering band of light. To the Eskimos it was a band of snow; to the Incas it was a trail of gold dust; to the Poly-nesians, a cloud-eating shark; and so on.

In 1750, Thomas Wright, an Englishman, proposed a modern model of the universe: the Milky Way was a thin disk of stars held between two spheres. If the sun were in the middle of the disk, one would see few stars at right angles to the disk, but along the disk one would see so many stars that they would blur together in a glowing band.

In 1775, the German philosopher Immanuel Kant elabo-rated on this model and imagined the individual stars to be like planets in a solar system. If this were so, they would all be swirling around the center of the Milky Way. He further reasoned that other collections of stars, which he called "Is-land universes," might exist farther out in the universe. Astronomers of that time had seen small, elliptical objects and had called them nebulous stars. Might these not be the island universes of Kant?

With an improved telescope that he built, William Her-schel, the Englishman who had discovered Uranus in 1781, began a systematic effort to map the universe. Herschel and his sister Caroline made extensive star counts in 683 differ-ent regions of the sky, and his conclusions confirmed Kant's idea of a disk-shaped Milky Way. In addition, Herschel's larg-er telescope resolved some of the "nebulous stars" into clusters of stars. He therefore proposed that some of these could be called other "milky ways."

By 1845, William Parson had used a 72-inch (1.8-meter) telescope to detect a distinct spiral structure in some of these distant star clusters, and this led to a renewal of interest in external galaxies. But the critical proof was missing. How to measure their distances? The technique of parallax works only for relatively close objects; it fails for these distant spiral objects.

Work on this problem led to one of the biggest revolutions in astronomy in the twentieth century. Astronomers proved conclusively that our galaxy is very large and that the sun is not at the center. This continued the revolution Copernicus started over four centuries before. Before astronomers could show other galaxies existed, they first had to determine how large our own galaxy is.

In the space of only 15 years, American astronomers determined the huge size of the Milky Way and showed that our galaxy is just one of billions of galaxies stretching across billions of light-years of space. They also discovered that space is expanding. As it does, it carries the galaxies with it, so they are moving apart. This in turn led scientists to seek answers to how the universe began.

THE MILKY WAY

Go out into the dark countryside some clear, moonless night in summer and you will see a hazy band of light stretched overhead. The Romans called it the *via lactea,* which translates as "milky way." What is it? How big is it? Where are the sun and Solar System in it?

These were the questions Harlow Shapley set out to answer in the early 1900s. Using the 60-inch (1.5-meter) telescope and later the new 100-inch (2.5-meter) telescope at the Mount Wilson Observatory, he began studying the distribution of globular clusters—gravitationally bound groups of many thousands of stars. He reasoned that since these are most often found away from the plane of the Milky Way, they might form a large, uniform, ball-like shell around the Milky Way.

Up until that time, most astronomers believed the sun was located in the middle of a flat disklike collection of stars which made up the plane of the Galaxy. Shapley found that most globular clusters were located in one direction, toward the constellation Sagittarius. When he completed a plot of the clusters' location, he made the daring suggestion that the Milky Way was at least 100,000 light-years across and that it contained as much mass as 200 billion suns. He also estimated that it was about 10,000 light-years thick and that the Solar System was about 30,000 light-years from the center. He was amazingly close to what we now believe to be the truth.

OTHER GALAXIES

At about the same time that Shapley was working, Edwin Hubble began studying an unusual class of objects called spiral nebulas. Some people had suggested that these were newly forming solar systems. Others believed they were the distant island universes Kant had written about. The real problem was to determine how far away they were. People had attempted to measure their distances using parallaxes but had failed. However, they still might be close enough to be a part of our galaxy.

An interesting discovery made by Henrietta Leavitt, an astronomer at Harvard College, helped Hubble out. While studying *Cepheid variables* (a type of variable star that changes its brightness) in a collection of stars called the Small Magellanic Cloud, she discovered that the brightest Cepheids took a long time (about 200 days) to go through their cycles. She also discovered that the dimmer ones took only a few days. This led to the formulation of her famous period-luminosity relationship or diagram.

Recall our earlier discussion of star brightness. Apparent magnitude is the brightness at which we actually see the star. Absolute magnitude is the brightness a star would have if it were 32.6 light-years away. If astronomers know both the absolute and apparent magnitudes of a star, they can easily find its distance.

Apparent magnitude is easily found from night-sky photographs. Henrietta Leavitt's period-luminosity diagram gave astronomers the absolute magnitude. They were now able to determine the distance not only to the Cepheid variables but also to the clusters and galaxies that contained them.

HUBBLE'S WORK

Using the same telescope as Shapley, Hubble began looking for Cepheid variables in the spiral "nebulas" (which is what he thought they were) M31 and M33 as well as in a third object called NGC 6822.* He gathered information for almost six years before he was ready to share his findings with other astronomers.

In each of these objects, he found the characteristic Cepheid variables. Most had long periods but appeared *dim*. Believing that "God doesn't play dice" with the universe (as Einstein later said), he concluded that the variable stars followed Leavitt's relationship, and therefore had to be at great distances from earth, so great that they could not be a part of our galaxy. He determined that both M31, in the constellation Andromeda, and M33, in Triangulum, were over 1 million light-years away. These are truly island universes. (Later it was found that these distances were still too small by a factor of two.)

OUR BIGGER AND BETTER GALAXY

What do we know about our galaxy today? First, we believe that it is a spiral galaxy with arms curled around its center. We still believe we are a long way from the center. We know our sun is located on the Orion spur between the Perseus

---

*Nonsteller objects that didn't seem to be stars were catalogued in the eighteenth century by the French astronomer Charles Messier. These were given Messier, or *M,* numbers (and sometimes names as well). In this century, astronomers have recatalogued Messier objects in another system—the New General Catalogue. These objects have *NGC* numbers. Because some objects are so well known by their Messier numbers, they are referred to here as such instead of by their NGC number.

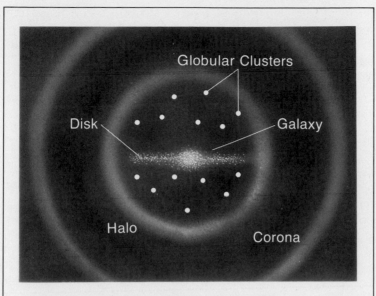

Diagram of Milky Way Galaxy surrounded
by halo of globular clusters.

arm and the Sagittarius arm. The Dutch astronomer Jan Oort
has shown that our sun orbits the Galaxy center once every
250 million years. This period is called the galactic year.

Bart Bok has been one of the most recent investigators
of the Milky Way's size and structure. His work, and the work
of others, suggests that we may have a bigger galaxy than
we earlier believed.

The work of Jeremiah Ostriker of Princeton University
and J. Einasto from Estonia, Soviet Union, has convinced
Bok that the Milky Way not only consists of a spiral disk and
shell of globular clusters but is surrounded by a vast coro-
na—or sphere—of some nonluminous material. This would
give our galaxy a mass of about two trillion times the mass of
the sun, ten times larger than we had previously believed.
Other astronomers have shown that the motions of the most
distant globular clusters around the Galaxy are such that the

mass of our galaxy must be at least 800 billion times the mass of our sun.

As a result, Bok estimated that our galaxy must be at least 300,000 light-years across and contain at least 800 billion solar masses. It truly is a bigger galaxy.

OTHER GALAXIES

In addition to proving that other galaxies existed, Hubble is credited with the first accepted galactic classification scheme. He noted that galaxies had either a spiral, an elliptical, or an irregular shape. He further noted that some spirals had a bar of stars through their center, while others had a spherical *nucleus,* or center. Today, however, newer schemes take into account galaxies that seem to have mixed characteristics.

NGC 6946, a spiral galaxy

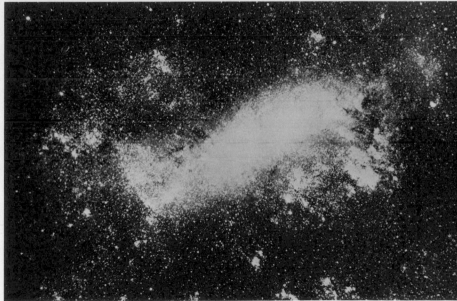

Above: NGC 135, an elliptical galaxy. Below: The Large Magellanic Cloud, an example of an irregular galaxy

For example, most elliptical galaxies contain no dark dust. But some (like NGC 5128) *do* have dark dust lanes across their thickest parts. We now call these "peculiar" galaxies. The study of such galaxies and other irregular galaxies has fascinated astronomers. The dark dust lane has a shattered appearance which suggests that a gigantic explosion may have occurred (or is still occurring) at the galactic center.

Another rare class of galaxies is the Seyfert galaxies. These are powerful emitters of X-rays and radio waves. All astronomers agree that some of this class (like NGC 1275) show filaments of gas light-years long, erupting from the center of a distorted galaxy. Some galaxies even seem to explode or at least have violent phases.

Recently astronomers have discovered another class of galaxies that does not fit Hubble's classification scheme, the ring galaxies. Large new telescopes fitted with devices that amplify the light from faint images have permitted astronomers to study fainter and fainter objects such as the ring galaxies.

These may be the result of a galactic collision with other galaxies. Galaxies do move, and in a universe made up of billions of them, once in a while they do run into each other. The process could take millions of years from collision to eventual formation of the ring.

BUNCHES OF GALAXIES

Astronomers quickly accepted the idea that galaxies existed. Soon they became curious as to whether galaxies exist in bunches. Hubble was one of the first to propose that galaxies typically are found in groups. Our own galaxy is a part of a small, irregular cluster of galaxies called the Local Group. This contains the Milky Way, the Andromeda galaxy, another spiral galaxy (M33), four irregular galaxies, and about twenty dwarf and regular elliptical galaxies. This group stretches about 4 million light-years across the sky.

Other galaxies are part of much larger clusters, some containing thousands of galaxies. These are called rich clusters. The late George Abell studied 2,712 rich clusters and found that some are spherical and some are not. One of the largest spherical clusters, the Coma Cluster, contains thousands of galaxies and is at least 10 million light-years across.

If galaxies come in clusters, do clusters of galaxies cluster into *super* clusters? Abell and another astronomer, Gerald de Voucouleurs, believed so. They found evidence for a Local Super Cluster that has a diameter of 100 million light-years and includes our Local Group, the Coma Cluster, and others. This super cluster contains at least a thousand trillion solar masses and appears to be flattened. This suggests that it may be rotating, but we really don't know. Abell found evidence of at least fifty more super clusters.

Work done at the Lick Observatory by William Shane and Carl Wirtanen has produced the first large-scale picture of the universe. They plotted one million bright galaxies. Their observations clearly suggest a clumpy, chainlike structure. This may be the imprint of the way the universe began. It may be evidence for the string theory of galaxy formation discussed in the next chapter.

If there are clusters of galaxies, and super clusters of galaxies, the next most obvious question is: "Is there evidence for a super-super clustering in the universe?" For the present, the answer is no. But it is a question still being investigated, whose answer may have to await new and more powerful tools. The present generation of telescopes, even with attached electronic devices, is limited in how far can be seen. The new generation of very large telescopes being planned and built, and the Hubble Space Telescope, will give us a deeper look at the universe.

CHAPTER 7
THE UNIVERSE
AT LARGE

*O*ne of the most exciting discoveries of the twentieth century is that the universe is expanding at a tremendous rate. This is deduced from the fact that for each 3.26 million light-years from us, all objects, including galaxies, are receding from us at a rate of about 38 miles per second (60 kilometers per second). How do we know this?

The story really began in 1912 when a young astronomer named Vesto Slipher was working at the Lowell Observatory in Flagstaff, Arizona. The director of the observatory, Percival Lowell, fascinated by the idea that spiral nebulas might be solar systems in formation, gave Slipher the difficult task of obtaining the spectra of these mysterious objects. By 1914, Slipher had obtained spectra for fourteen of them. What he found astonished the astronomers of that day. The spectra were the same as if they were from a group of stars. But the real surprise was that the spectral lines did not show up where one would expect. They were all shifted to the long-wavelength end of the spectrum.

Slipher found that *light* from a star or group of stars moving away from earth has *its* waves lengthened, too. Since the red end of the spectrum is made up of longer wavelengths of light, astronomers call this displacement of spectral lines a *redshift*. On the other hand, if the light is coming from a star speeding toward you, the effect is just the opposite—a blue shift. These shifts are also known as Doppler shifts (see Chapter 2).

Not only can you tell whether an object is moving toward or away from you, you can measure how fast it is moving. Slipher found that his nebulas were receding at many miles

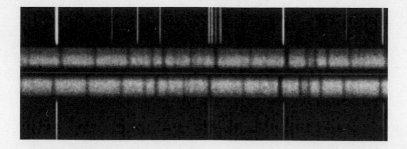

An example of the Doppler shift. Each set of dark lines represents part of the spectrum of a star; the lines indicate the presence of light of a certain wavelength. The bright lines are reference lines: they show where the lines should be for a nonmoving object. In this picture, the top set of dark lines is shifted to the right, indicating a redshift: the star is moving away from a viewer on earth. The bottom set of lines indicates a blueshift: the star is moving toward a viewer on earth. It so happens that these are the spectra of a binary star. Try to imagine a pair of stars rotating about each other in such a manner that one of the stars is always moving away from us while the other is moving toward us.

(or kilometers) per second! When he presented his results to the American Astronomical Society, the astronomers stood up and applauded. This is very unusual at a scientific meeting. They realized that Slipher had made an important discovery, but they didn't really understand it. At that time we still hadn't even proved that other galaxies existed. We know now that Slipher was showing that galaxies are receding from us at high velocities.

HUBBLE'S WORK

Then, as a result of having a larger telescope (the Mount Wilson 100-inch, or 2.5-meter), Edwin Hubble used the period-luminosity law and was able to show that these spiral nebulas are at immense distances from the Milky Way. They really are other island universes.

By 1929, Hubble had obtained the distances for eighteen galaxies and used Slipher's work on velocities to show that galactic distances and velocities were related. The farther a galaxy is from the earth, the *faster* it is receding. What's more, if a galaxy is twice as far away, it is receding *twice* as fast. If it is three times as far away, it is receding *three* times as fast, and so on. This led to the idea that the universe is expanding.

But expanding from what? If you drive in a straight line so that you are 100 miles (160 kilometers) from home and drive 50 miles per hour (80 kilometers per hour), and your friend drives in another direction for 50 miles (80 kilometers) at 25 miles per hour (40 kilometers per hour), and you both start out at the same time from the same place, you can calculate *when* you both left. It would have been two hours ago, of course.

Astronomers reasoned that the age of the universe could be calculated in the same way. Most astronomers now agree that the universe began with a *big bang* about 13 to 18 billion years ago.

THE BIG BANG:
A UNIVERSE IS BORN

Starting in the 1930s, astronomers began investigating the birth of the universe. The big bang theory said that the universe began with a violent explosion and started the expansion we still see today. The rapidly expanding matter cooled and broke up into clouds of gas. These formed the galaxies.

If we trace this explosion back in time to the beginning, we can predict that the "cosmic egg"—the "lump" of matter that exploded—was very dense and very hot, perhaps 2 trillion degrees Fahrenheit (1 trillion degrees Celsius). What would it be like to be there? First, you would be surrounded by very dense, hot blobs of energy. (You would only be such a blob yourself!) In the first few seconds after the big bang, the temperature would drop to about 2 billion degrees Fahrenheit (1 billion degrees Celsius), and in about two to three minutes, the first atoms would form. Only the light elements, hydrogen and helium, can be built under these conditions. That is why the universe today is made up of mostly these two elements.

Astronomers have trouble explaining how galaxies formed. We know they did, but probably not until millions of years after the big bang. One of the recent very speculative ideas was proposed in 1981 by the astronomer Alex Vilenkin. He suggested that the powerful forces of the big bang would produce long thin tubes of energy, which he calls *strings*. These would be thinner than atoms, yet the mass of just 1 inch (2.5 centimeters) of string would equal the mass of a large chain of mountains.

These strings would wander through the early universe. They would move through the blobs of gas, distorting the smooth structure and making dense pockets that would cool and form galaxies. These strings would pull in so much matter that the string would collapse and form a black hole.

Does this mean that every galaxy should have a black hole in its center? Radio astronomers think there is something strange and powerful in the center of our Milky Way. During the 1970s Robert Haymas from Rice University in Texas used a balloon-borne instrument carrying a gamma ray telescope to study the center of our galaxy. He discovered that the galactic center produced a hundred thousand times as much energy in a single wavelength as the sun in all wavelengths! This led the Caltech astronomer Donald Lynden-Bell to call this "the beast at the center of the Galaxy."

WHAT IS THIS BEAST?

Later work has mapped the center of our galaxy with radio telescopes. The whole area is called Sagittarius-A, and part of it is a large cloud of hot gas. Another part is a small object (just how small we don't know) that may be our beast. The beast may be a black hole pulling in gas and producing radiation. It may be a massive black hole eating up stars from a surrounding cluster of stars. What we do know is that other galaxies, like the giant elliptical galaxy M87, also have something massive and strange in their centers that many astronomers believe are black holes. Don't forget the exploding galaxies like NGC 1275 mentioned in the last chapter. Could a black hole cause such an explosion? It's tempting to think so, but we really don't know.

OTHER EVIDENCE FOR
THE BIG BANG

If the universe really did begin with a hot big bang, shouldn't we be able to measure the temperature of the "cooling embers," or radio signals, left over from the moment of birth? The physicist George Gamow predicted in the late 1940s that we ought to be able to. Finally, in the 1960s Arno Penzias and Robert Wilson, working for the Bell Laboratories in New Jersey, did just that.

Using a specially shaped radio telescope, they detected a uniform background radio hiss from every direction in the universe. At first they didn't know what it meant, but when Robert Dicke at Princeton University heard of their finding, he quickly pointed out the true nature of their discovery.

M87, a galaxy that appears to be ejecting material

If the big bang occurred a long time ago, its radiation would be so redshifted that we would pick it up in the radio part of the electromagnetic spectrum. It should come from all directions in the universe. Penzias and Wilson had discovered the background radio signals of the big bang just as had been predicted. This was the final proof that the universe began as astronomers had deduced. In 1978, Penzias and Wilson were awarded the Nobel prize for this important discovery.

WHAT IS THE FATE OF THE UNIVERSE?

Astronomers support one of two answers to this question: (1) The universe will expand forever, with the stars and galaxies eventually dying out. (2) The universe will slow its expansion, stop, then collapse in a "big crunch." This would happen when all matter in the universe piled back up on itself. In order for the big crunch to occur, there has to be enough mass to produce enough gravity to slow and stop the expansion.

At the present, astronomers cannot find enough visible matter in the universe to support the latter hypothesis. When we add up all the *visible* matter in the universe, we can't find enough to stop the expansion we observe. But there are mysteries that we can't explain.

We see huge clusters of galaxies that seem to group together for billions of years, yet the individual galaxies are moving so fast that most of them should have escaped the combined gravity of the group. What does this mean? Maybe there are large amounts of mass that we *can't* see. Maybe it is in the form of black holes.

Other astronomers suggest that neutrinos may make up the "missing mass." A *neutrino* is a tiny subatomic particle, with neutral charge and supposedly no mass, traveling at the speed of light. Billions have sped through your body while you read the previous sentence. Perhaps, these other astronomers are saying, the neutrino does have a tiny mass—extremely tiny. Since they are so numerous, the total mass becomes significant and could easily account for the "missing mass." This is being investigated with some exotic experiments in the Soviet Union, Japan, Italy, and the United States.

POWERHOUSES IN THE SKY

As has happened many times in the history of astronomy, the use of a new tool leads to new information and new discoveries. The discovery of quasars is just one example.

Following World War II, astronomers were given a number of surplus radar sets. These were put to work "listening" to the sky using radio waves. One of the first radio sky surveys to be completed was in Cambridge, England, where radio astronomers in the late 1950s discovered a number of powerful, natural radio sources. Some were on or in huge clouds of gas. Others seemed located in the center of the Milky Way.

The exact location of some of these strong beacons is hard to determine. When radio telescopes are used alone, they are nearsighted. The later use of multiple radio telescopes separated by large distances and hooked together by computers solved the problem of pinpointing these sources. This technique, called interferometry, was discussed earlier.

Two bright starlike objects called 3C 48 and 3C 273 were soon identified as the source of these strong radio signals. (These numbers are listings in the *Third Cambridge Catalog of Radio Sources*.) Astronomers were puzzled. Ordinary stars, like the sun, don't produce strong radio noise. Astronomers coined a new name for these unusual objects—"quasi-stellar objects," *quasars*, for short.

UNLOCKING PART OF THE MYSTERY

In 1963, Maarten Schmidt and Jesse Greenstein, both working at the California Institute of Technology, unlocked part of the secret of quasars, only to open a new mystery.

They found a very large redshift in the spectra of 3C 48 and 3C 273. Using Hubble's law, this meant the quasars were very far away. For example, 3C 273 is estimated to be 3 bil-

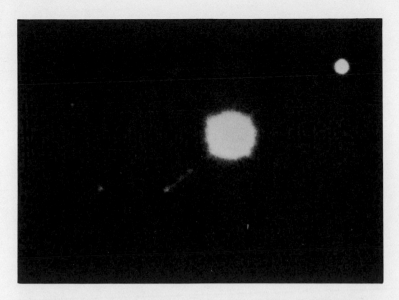

3C 273 (in the center), a quasar in the constellation Virgo

lion light-years away. Oddly, quasars are also very luminous—in fact, more luminous than most galaxies. They also
found that there were no *close* quasars. The closest known
quasar is 3C 273.

At first astronomers couldn't believe that these objects
were really that far away. For one thing, they found that the
quasars varied their energy output in just a few weeks or
years. This meant they really weren't as big as galaxies. The
recent discovery of multiple quasars has convinced most
astronomers that we are seeing distant, small, and powerful
energy sources.

In 1979, Dennis Walsh, Robert F. Carswell, and Ray J.
Weymann discovered that a pair of quasars (known collec-
tively as 0975+561) had similar appearances and identical
redshifts. These astronomers suggested that we were really
seeing *two* images of the same quasar produced by an inter-
vening *gravitational lens.*

Large, massive objects (like galaxies) actually bend
space. If a distant galaxy just happened to be between us

and a quasar, the light from the quasar would be bent into two or more paths. We would see the quasar twice! This phenomenon is called a gravitational lens. Albert Einstein had predicted just such a phenomenon in his general theory of relativity.

In 1980, a team of astronomers at the Palomar Observatory found a normal 18th-magnitude galaxy in the same line of sight as this pair of quasars. The redshift of this galaxy is only about a third that of the quasar. The position and estimated mass of this galaxy would produce the gravitational lens effect. Other cases like this have been found.

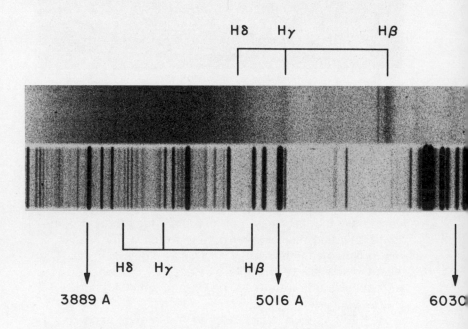

Part of the spectrum of the quasar 3C 273 (top). The bottom spectrum is shown here for comparison. Note the positions of the three marked spectral lines in each spectrum. The lines in the top spectrum are shifted to the right. Most astronomers believe the shift indicates that quasars are very far from earth and receding from earth at tremendous speeds.

WHAT ARE QUASARS?

Here is a list of some of the things we know about quasars:

1. The energy region of a quasar is quite small compared with that of a galaxy.
2. Quasars are all quite distant, meaning we are seeing them as they were a long time ago. There are no close, recent quasars.
3. Some quasars have jets of material coming out of them.
4. Quasars radiate all types of energy: light, X-rays, and radio. The total energy represents more than a *hundred* times the output of a galaxy.
5. Some quasars have been determined to have a "fuzz" around them that has the spectra of normal stars. Bruce Campbell of the Dominion Astrophysical Observatory in Canada recently discovered a supernova in quasar QSO 1059+130. (QSO stands for quasi-stellar object.) These two facts suggest that quasars are surrounded by normal stars.
6. We detect the spectra of hot gases in quasars.

From these facts, astronomers have built a "mental model" of a quasar: Quasars have a compact central energy source, perhaps a giant black hole equal in mass to a hundred billion suns. If this black hole swallowed about as much mass per year as found in a typical star, it could produce as much energy as we measure from a quasar. This energy comes out in the form of X-rays and visible light. Some of the material being pulled in heats up and glows to produce the spectra of a hot gas.

It is tempting to believe we are seeing a galaxy in formation. This would explain the absence of nearby quasars.

But what formed the central powerhouse originally? How do the massive black holes (if that is what they are) form in the first place? Work now being done on the string theory of the universe may provide answers to these questions. Astronomers will have to use new tools and new ideas to solve these and other mysteries of the universe.

CHAPTER 8
LOOKING
FOR E.T.

*F*or several million years, our ancestors have looked upward, wondering about the nature of the lights visible in the night sky. Gradually, during the last 2,000 years, we have come to understand that we are looking at planets, stars, galaxies, and other objects in the heavens. But with this understanding has come a new question: Are we alone? Do intelligent creatures exist on those planets, near those stars, or within those galaxies?

This is a question that we finally have the ability to try to answer. A growing number of scientists are working on the problem in a variety of ways. But before we can discuss these ways, we need to examine life on the one place we know it exists—earth.

THE ORIGIN OF
LIFE ON EARTH

Life, as we know it, consists of organisms that can grow and reproduce themselves. Since living things are largely constructed from complex strings of carbon atoms linked with other elements, we have come to refer to life on this planet as carbon based. This is the only kind of life we know. The other molecule necessary for life is water. All the plants, animals, and other organisms of this world are composed mostly of water. Our own bodies are three-quarters water. No living organism can exist without water. This is a clue to where life on this planet began—in the oceans.

Soon after our planet collected itself from the gas and dust surrounding the newly formed sun, earth was a hot and lifeless world. Eventually, it cooled enough for the moisture held in the atmosphere to rain down upon the surface to form the first seas.

In 1953, the chemists Stanley Miller and Harold Urey performed a series of experiments that attempted to reproduce the conditions of this early earth, to see what might happen. Water was placed in a flask along with the other gases thought to compose the earth's primitive atmosphere: ammonia, methane, and hydrogen. An electric spark to simulate lightning was discharged in the flask. After allowing the experiment to run a week, the scientists found that *amino acids* had been produced.

Amino acids are not alive, but they are the first step along the way toward life. They form the basis for proteins, the fundamental building blocks of living matter.

More recently, in 1969, scientists discovered that some meteorites contained amino acids. It is possible, then, that the first amino acids on this planet might have even originated in outer space.

Regardless of how amino acids got here, within a few million years of their development or arrival, the earth's oceans, teeming with organic molecules, probably resembled a thin, foul-smelling soup.

The real mystery of this whole process is the next step. How did this sea of organic molecules manage to produce living cells—microorganisms? We don't know. Maybe it was a natural occurrence, the result of the way organic molecules interact with one another. Or perhaps it was a truly nonreproducible event, which could never be repeated on any other planet of the galaxy. Somehow, though, it did happen.

The fossil record indicates that about 3.5 billion years ago, the first microorganisms appeared. From these humble beginnings, increasingly more complex organisms were generated. Eventually not only the sea, but also the land and the air were populated. Our primitive ancestors came on the scene late in the game, "only" 3 to 4 million years ago. But once the development of intelligence came about, life in this corner of the universe would never be the same. Now we wonder if there is anything like us elsewhere in the universe, and we build the tools to make the search.

OUR SOLAR SYSTEM

We began the search by looking in our own backyard—the other planets and moons of our Solar System. All scientists agree that the most similar environment to earth (within our Solar System) is found on Mars. It may not be the best place to spend a summer vacation, but with a little fixing up, human beings could live there.

Viking 1 and *2* were sent to Mars in 1976 to look for possible life. Although no obvious life forms were photographed, life still might exist in the form of microorganisms in the soil, or traces of previous life might be detected. As a result, a series of experiments involving Martian soil, water, and nutrients was performed.

Today, most scientists agree that the *Viking* spacecraft detected no signs of life on Mars, though it did find some unusual soil chemistry. This does not mean that life does not or did not exist anywhere on Mars. But it makes us rather pessimistic. Our best candidate for life within the Solar System seems unpromising.

Some scientists claim that we have only scratched the surface. Carl Sagan points to the clouds of Jupiter as a possible abode for airborn life. The famous British astronomer Fred Hoyle claims that the cores of comets might be warm enough to melt, creating lakes in which simple life might exist. Other scientists want to examine the oceans of Jupiter's moon Europa or Saturn's moon Titan for possible life.

Though these places, and others, are worthy of consideration, it is becoming apparent that any life found elsewhere in our Solar System is likely to be simple life—not intelligent. What about life on objects beyond our Solar System?

OTHER PLANETARY SYSTEMS

Astronomers have been hunting for planets orbiting other stars for more than a century. Unfortunately, they have met with little success. The reason can be seen from the following.

Pluto, the farthest known planet, is visible only when viewed through a large telescope under normal conditions.

The nearest stars are tens of thousands of times further away than Pluto. Imagine the difficulty of looking for a faint planet at these distances, especially when a fairly bright star is close to the planet and you are looking through our own shimmering atmosphere. With current ground-based telescopes, catching a view of planets in another star system is impossible.

However, there are other ways to search. The American astronomer Peter van de Kamp announced after a decade-long study of several nearby stars that a few show a wobble in their motions as they move through space. This could be caused by orbiting planets. Although his findings have been questioned, other astronomers have been encouraged to seek new methods to detect planets.

The infrared satellite IRAS has located several nearby stars surrounded by infrared emission. Astronomers believe that this emission comes from dust and gas clouds that surround these stars. These clouds are material left over from the star's formation. Astronomers hypothesize that such clouds will form (or in some cases have already formed) planetary systems.

A group of astronomers at the University of Arizona used a new technique to carefully search the area around the nearby star Beta Pictoris in 1984. They discovered a disk of material seen nearly edge-on. They believe this is dust left over after planets formed around Beta Pictoris.

It is beginning to appear that other stars (perhaps many other stars) have planetary systems. If this is so, we have our possible abodes for life. But how might we detect such possible life?

SPACE PROBES?

Space is a big place. Sending a space probe out into this dark ocean is a lot like dropping a note in a bottle into the sea. The fastest space probe we have ever launched was the *Pioneer 10* probe in 1972, and seventeen years were needed for it to reach the orbit of Pluto. To reach even the nearest of stars would take tens of thousands of years.

Yet scientists did attach messages to *Pioneer 10* and its

The "sounds of earth" videodisc aboard Voyager 2.
*The record is made of gold-plated copper and
contains sounds, music, pictures, and a message
from former president Jimmy Carter.*

sister probe *Pioneer 11.* The small plaques, which look like
metal postcards, show a man and woman standing in front of
a drawing of the spacecraft. There is also a drawing of our
Solar System and some data about where we are located
and when the probe was launched.

Five years later, the messages placed on the *Voyager 1*
and *2* probes were a bit more sophisticated. Each contained
a gold video disk along with instructions on how to use it to
reproduce the sights and sounds of earth.

In all likelihood the spacecraft and their messages will

never be found by aliens. If anyone does find them, it may be our own descendants overtaking them as they journey outward. (Remember the movie *Star Trek I*?) Perhaps the craft and plaque will wind up in some twenty-fourth-century museum as relics of a nearly forgotten past.

INTERSTELLAR TRAVEL

A better way to contact extraterrestrial life may be for humans to make the journey themselves. Here there are two options: a slow, inexpensive trip, or a quick, expensive trip.

The slow, inexpensive option would involve launching a traveling space colony. (Here we use the term "inexpensive" to refer to the fuel requirements. In truth, the undertaking would be financially quite expensive.) A huge starship, containing hundreds if not thousands of people, would be launched on a leisurely flight toward Alpha Centauri. At 30 miles per second (50 kilometers per second), the escape velocity for our Solar System, the trip would take about 27,000 years. Obviously, the people who began the journey would not arrive at their destination, but their descendants just might—that is, if all the engineering and social problems along the way could be solved.

The other option, that of a quick flight, would be unbelievably expensive in terms of the energy required. The quickest way to get from one place to another is to accelerate halfway there and to decelerate the last halfway. This is like saying the quickest way to get from one stoplight to the next is to "floor" the accelerator and then jam on the brakes as you get to your stop.

Suppose we accelerate a small spaceship at 32 feet per second per second (9.8 meters per second per second) toward Alpha Centauri. Its maximum velocity would be about 90 percent of the speed of light. Halfway there we begin decelerating by the same amount. We could make the round trip within a person's lifetime, but the amount of fuel required would be enormous. Such a journey probably will remain an invention of science fiction for the foreseeable future. Another problem is gamma and X-ray radiation created by the impact of the spaceship with interstellar gas at greater than half the speed of light. Their radiation is lethal.

SEARCHING BY RADIO

Perhaps the best, if not the only, option we have for finding life elsewhere is something we are already trying—looking by radio. We have been listening to the stars for more than half a century. Although we have learned a lot about the universe, so far we have not overheard anyone from another world.

More than a dozen studies have been made since the first modern attempt in 1960 by the American astronomer Frank Drake, who pointed an 86-foot (26-meter) radio dish in Green Bank, West Virginia, toward two nearby stars for 150 hours. Although these searches have failed, only a few hundred stars have been examined. The problem is not only picking the right star, but also finding the right radio frequency and the right time. The negative findings are not too surprising.

Although it is more practical for us to listen for signals than to send them (for the same reason that it is cheaper to make a radio receiver than to build a radio station), occasionally radio signals have been beamed to the stars. One time was in 1974 when the huge radio telescope in Arecibo, Puerto Rico, was resurfaced to improve its sensitivity. At that time, a powerful signal was beamed toward the globular cluster of stars (M13) in the constellation Hercules. The message was a series of dots and dashes that could be reconstructed into a picture. It showed the human form, the DNA molecule, the Solar System, the radio dish, and other data.

If anyone out there was listening, they might have noticed a three-minute blast of radio energy containing the message coming from our area of the sky. But we'll have to be patient for any possible reply: the cluster is 24,000 light-years away. That means that if we do get an answer, it should be about the year A.D. 50,000.

HAS E.T. ALREADY BEEN HERE?

The subject of UFOs is one that tends to polarize people. Either you believe they represent visits by extraterrestrials, or you believe they are hoaxes or misidentified natural or human-made phenomena. Few people have no opinion on the subject.

The scientific community is solidly in favor of the view that there is no good evidence that UFOs are extraterrestrial spacecraft. This is not to say that these same scientists do not believe in the likelihood of extraterrestrials. Many insist that the universe is so vast that it seems highly improbable that we are the only intelligent species that exists.

All too often, UFO reports can be readily attributed to bright stars, meteors, clouds, ball lightning, flocks of birds, helicopters, balloons, or satellites, to name a few phenomena. The few cases that do not fall into these categories usually happen in peculiar circumstances. They never occur in broad daylight with hundreds of witnesses. Usually there are only one or two observers in poor lighting, and the only proof is an ambiguous photograph.

It seems incredible that among the one group of people trained to observe the skies, there has never been a reported sighting of an alien spacecraft. Thousands of professional and amateur astronomers study the heavens each night without any such sightings. Thousands of amateur radio operators are constantly scanning all radio frequencies 24 hours a day. They have heard nothing from an extraterrestrial spacecraft. This strongly argues that UFOs are not the products or manifestations of extraterrestrial intelligence.

The universe is a huge and marvelous place. Events considered part of the realm of fantasy a generation ago are being witnessed today; objects unimaginable then have become accepted as reality today. As yet, however, extraterrestrial life has not been found.

GLOSSARY

Absolute magnitude—The brightness a star would have if it were a standard distance away (32.6 light-years); used for comparison.

Absolute zero—The lowest possible temperature (-459 degrees Fahrenheit, or -273 degrees Celsius, or 0 degrees Kelvin), at which all atomic and molecular movement ceases.

Amino acid—Carbon-chain molecules that are the building blocks of protein.

Apollo asteroid—One of a group of asteriods whose orbits cross the earth's orbit.

Apparent magnitude—The actual brightness of a star as seen by human eyes from earth.

Asteroid—One of thousands of small, irregular bodies orbiting the sun, found mostly between the orbits of Mars and Jupiter.

Big bang—According to the theory of the same name, the violent explosion that formed the universe we know.

Binary stars—A double-star system in which the two stars orbit a common center of mass.

Black hole—The object that results when a star has collapsed under the force of its own gravity to the point that nothing, not even light, can escape from it.

Cepheid variable—A type of supergiant pulsating star that oscillates in brightness over periods from one to one hundred days. The period length is linked to the absolute magnitude by a known relationship.

Comet—An object made of ice and rocky material that may orbit the sun regularly or just pass it once. As it enters the ·

inner Solar System, it warms and the vaporized gases form a glowing head and an extended tail.

Doppler effect—Synonymous with Doppler shift.

Doppler shift—A shift in the wavelength of light and all electromagnetic radiation from an object due to the object's motion. Motion toward the observer shortens the wavelength (blueshift), and motion away from the observer lengthens the wavelength (redshift).

Eclipse—The cutting off of all or part of the light of one body by another passing in front of it.

Electromagnetic radiation—Radiant energy consisting of particles, called photons, with different wavelengths. Each photon is formed of magnetic and electric fields.

Electromagnetic spectrum—The term for all the wavelengths of electromagnetic radiation from the shortest wavelengths of gamma rays to the longest wavelengths of radio waves. Starting with the longest wavelength the sequence is: radio, infrared, visible, ultraviolet, X-ray, and gamma.

Gamma rays—Radiation of extremely short wavelengths. The most energetic portion of the electromagnetic spectrum.

Gravitational lens—A massive celestial object that curves the space near it, causing the path of light to bend. This results in multiple images of the same body, usually a quasar.

Infrared radiation—Long-wavelength radiation that produces heat energy when absorbed by matter.

Interferometry—A technique in which two or more telescopes are used together to produce the resolving power of one large telescope.

Light-year—The distance a beam of light travels in one year, or approximately 6 trillion miles (9.5 trillion kilometers).

M—Used to identify certain types of astronomical objects, such as nebulas; for example, M31. M stands for Messier object, after the French astronomer Charles Messier, who cataloged these objects.

Maria—(MAR-ee-ah)—large, flat plains, first seen on the moon by Galileo and originally believed to be seas.

Meteor—The flash of one or two seconds' duration when a meteoroid, plunging into the earth's atmosphere, is incandescently vaporized.

Meteorite—A large meteoroid that has reached the earth's surface because it was not completely vaporized during the meteor phase.

Meteoroid—Any object in space destined to encounter the earth's atmosphere.

Nebula—A cloud of dust and gas in space.

Neutrino—A tiny subatomic particle with neutral electric charge and supposedly no mass, traveling at or near the speed of light.

Neutron star—The remaining core of a massive star after the supernova phase. It consists of closely packed neutrons and is about 13 miles (20 kilometers) in diameter. A neutron star is extremely dense and spins rapidly.

NGC—New General Catalog listing; a catalog of nebulas and star clusters.

Nova—A star that suddenly brightens by a factor of five to fifteen magnitudes or more. Believed to occur when a dwarf is part of a binary system and is pulling gas from an extended red giant partner.

Nucleus (plural: nuclei)—(1) the core of a comet; (2) the core of an atom; (3) the core of a galaxy.

Parallax—An apparent shift in the position of an object when observed from two different places, such as from the earth six months apart. Used to measure astronomical distances.

Perihelion—The point in an object's orbit closest to the sun.

Pulsar—A rapidly rotating neutron star that emits a beam of radio waves (and sometimes light waves). By means of the lighthouse effect, these are detected as pulses.

Quasar—A starlike object that generates enormous amounts of energy. Also termed QSO, quasi-stellar object.

Radio telescope—A radio receiver built to listen to radio emissions from the heavens, usually with a huge reflector dish.

Red giant—A stage in the lifetime of certain stars in which the outer layers of the star expand, becoming so "cool" that the color of the light reddens. Our sun will become a red giant in about 5 billion years.

Redshift—A shift in the wavelength of an object's light or other radiation toward the longer wavelengths. Caused by movement away from the observer. The universal red shift of all galaxies is evidence of the expanding universe.

Resolution—A measure of the ability of a telescope to separate two sources of radiation into two distinct images.

Solar wind—A stream of charged particles flowing away from the sun.

Spectrograph—A device that spreads the light from an object into its various colors or wavelengths and then photographs the resulting spectrum.

Spectroscope—A device used to form a spectrum from the radiation emitted by a luminous object.

Spectrum (plural: spectra)—A display of electromagnetic radiation spread out by wavelength.

Stellar evolution—The gradual changes of a star's characteristics from birth as a contracting gas cloud to end as a white dwarf, neutron star, or black hole.

Strings—A theoretical construct developed in an attempt to explain the formation of galaxies; they are thin but extremely massive and long.

Subatomic particle—One of the many particles involved in the structure of the atom; the electron, proton, and neutron are the most stable.

Sublimate—To change phases by passing directly from a solid to a gas by evaporation without passing through the liquid phase. Dry ice (frozen carbon dioxide) sublimates.

Supernova—The explosive destruction of a massive star which occurs when the star exhausts all of its nuclear fuel. A supernova is never recurrent, whereas a nova is. A supernova leaves behind a neutron star or a black hole.

Ultraviolet radiation—Short-wavelength radiation, just shorter than visible violet light; the component of sunlight that causes tanning.

White dwarf—The final stage of evolution of a "lightweight" star such as our sun; about the size of the earth and the mass of the sun.

X-radiation—See X-rays.

X-rays—Energetic, penetrating electromagnetic radiation with wavelengths shorter than ultraviolet rays. Emitted by gas when heated to millions of degrees (Fahrenheit or Celsius).

SELECTED READING

Apfel, Necia H. *Stars and Galaxies.* New York: Franklin Watts, 1982.

Asimov, Isaac. *Venus, Near Neighbor of the Sun.* New York: Lothrop, Lee, and Shepard, 1981.

Beatty, J. Kelly, et. al. *The New Solar System.* Cambridge, Mass.: Sky Publishing, 1982.

Berger, Melvin. *Bright Stars, Red Giants and White Dwarfs.* New York: G.P. Putnam's Sons, 1983.

Branley, Franklyn M. *Mysteries of Outer Space.* New York: Lodestar Books, 1985.

Ford, Adam. *Spaceship Earth.* New York: Lothrop, Lee, and Shepard, 1981.

Friedman, Herbert. *The Amazing Universe.* Washington, D.C.: National Geographic Society, 1975.

Gallant, Roy A. *The Planets.* New York: Four Winds Press, 1982.

Henbest, Nigel and Michael Marten. *The New Astronomy.* Cambridge, England: Cambridge University Press, 1983.

Jacobs, Francine. *Cosmic Countdown.* New York: M. Evans and Company, 1983.

Lauber, Patricia. *Journey to the Planets.* New York: Crown, 1982.

Littman, Mark and Donald K. Yocmons. *Comet Halley: Once in a Lifetime.* Washington, D.C.: American Chemical Society, 1985.

Pasachoff, Jay M. *Contemporary Astronomy.* Third edition. Philadelphia: Saunders, 1985.

Traister, Robert J. and Susan E. Harris. *Astronomy and Telescopes: A Beginners Handbook.* Blue Ridge Summit, Penn.: Tab Books, 1983.

Vogt, Gregory. *Mars and the Inner Planets.* New York: Franklin Watts, 1982.

INDEX